"*Tango Noir* is riveting in its sensuality and theatricality."
~ Joyce Doolittle, *NeWest Review*

"*Bête Blanche* curls itself around the listener like a cool white drape on a close July night. It is tantalizing and thoroughly engrossing, a near perfect production in every respect."
~ Colin Snowsell, *The Weal*

"*Tango Noir* is witty, artful and literate, finding Calgary playwright Scollard at her best. Director Gerri Hemphill comes close to approximating the shifting moods of a dream world, colouring certain moments with Kevin Labchuk's brooding musical score, which slips in quietly, builds and then abruptly vanishes. And a central scene in which Henri's Colette and Collette's Mata Hari slowly apply makeup to their faces is entrancing."
~ Martin Morrow, *The Calgary Herald*.

D0926318

Tango Noir

Three plays by Rose Scollard

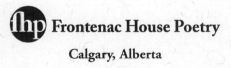 Frontenac House Poetry

Calgary, Alberta

Book and cover design: Epix Design
Cover Image: David Scollard

Library and Archives Canada Cataloguing in Publication

Scollard, Rose
Tango noir : three plays / Rose Scollard.

Plays.
issued also in electronic format

ISBN 978-1-897181-44-7

I.   Title.

PS8587.C615T35 2012   C812'.54   C2012-906694-X

We acknowledge the support of the Canada Council for the Arts for
our publishing program. We also acknowledge The Alberta Multimedia
Development Fund for their support of our publishing program.

 Canada Council **Conseil des Arts**
for the Arts **du Canada**

**Government
of Alberta** ■

Printed and bound in Canada
Published by Frontenac House
1138 Frontenac Ave. SW
Calgary, Alberta, T2T 1B6, Canada
Tel: 403-245-8588
www.frontenachouse.com

For David

Contents

Bête Blanche

Bête Blanche/Tango Noir was produced at the
Pumphouse in Calgary, April 1991.

Bête Blanche
Faye   Alexandria Patience
Cliff / Shadow   Don Enright

Tango Noir
Marguerite / Colette [Scene Two]   Alexandria Patience
Colette [Scene One] /   Don Enright
Captain Bouchardon /
Sister Maria / Henri

Director   Gerri Hemphill
Set and Lighting Design   Sandi Somers
Costume Design   Lillian Messer
Choreography   Nicole Mion
Waltz, Tango and Soundscape   Kevin Labchuk
Stage Manager   Nancy Jo Cullen

Characters

This play is for two actors:

A woman who plays
FAYE

And a man who plays
CLIFF and SHADOW

Setting: Calgary, 1935

~~~~~~~~~~~~~~~~~~~~~~~~~~~~~~~~~~~~~

[Dim spot on a large portmanteau placed prominently on a chair in a living room. It is a room where people live close to the bone – a chair, a lamp, a table, a worn rug – no extras.

FAYE *enters. Curses the dark.]*

FAYE: Damned electric! Cliff!

[She fumbles about in a drawer, brings out a candle. Lighting it, she sees the portmanteau, reflects a momentary spark of interest, then fixes her face. But, in spite of herself, FAYE *is attracted to the bag. She goes to it, opens it and takes out what she is obviously looking for: a wallet. Aware of someone beyond, she searches through it and removes three one-dollar bills.* FAYE *replaces the wallet and, idly fumbling through the bag, to her surprise finds something else. It is a man's dressing case, expensive and beautifully made of tooled Moroccan leather. Inside, the fittings are of silver, tarnished but solid. She fingers and turns over each piece: the razor, the brushes, a scent bottle. She rubs the lid of a jar and is startled by something she imagines is inside it. She examines the jar and works at the lid. When she opens it there is a shifting sound somewhere in the room.]*

FAYE: Who is that? Cliff?

[She looks about uneasily and stuffs the case back in the bag but, thinking better of it, removes the case and hides it in the room.

Again her attention is drawn and she looks harder into the gloom. Then, hearing a sound offstage, she sits at the table and riffles through a magazine.

Door opens and CLIFF *stands in the doorway, holding a book.]*

FAYE: *[Reading from her magazine, wearily.]* "The door opened and her husband stood uncertainly in the doorway. Framed by the kitchen light he could have been the very one who had captured her young imagination – tall, lean, the kind who could wear open-necked shirts and tweeds, puff philosophically on a pipe and still come off looking like a man."

*[*CLIFF, *looking like the kind of man* FAYE *is reading about, goes to the portmanteau.]*

CLIFF: Faye? I've decided, Faye.

FAYE: I saw the bag. *[*CLIFF *opens the bag and, without looking at the contents, puts the book inside.]*

FAYE: Cliff? Was there someone in the house just now?

CLIFF: Here?

FAYE: I thought I saw someone. A white figure, perfume and fur.

CLIFF: A woman?

FAYE: I don't know. It was just an impression. You know, out of the side of my eye.

CLIFF: You must have dozed off for a minute.

FAYE: Yes.

[They both look at the bag, an awkward moment.]

CLIFF: I'm going to give the cars a try. There's one going out at five.

FAYE: Five. That's early, isn't it?

*[*CLIFF *stands tentatively beside* FAYE, *hands in pockets. He is hunched in a way that suggests anxiety but* FAYE *seems to feel no obligation to soothe or praise him. He unpockets a hand and places*

it on her arm; then, aware of her subtle stiffening, slips it off again.]

CLIFF: I thought I'd snatch a couple of hours sleep before I left. I won't waken the boys.

FAYE: That's probably wise.

CLIFF: You'll say goodbye to them for me?

FAYE: Sure.

CLIFF: I have a little something for you. Not much, but it should cover an emergency if the dole doesn't come through right away.

[FAYE takes the offered money and starts to leaf through it.]

CLIFF: It's only six dollars.

FAYE: You sold your watch, didn't you. You sap.

CLIFF: You've been on to me to sell it for a month now.

FAYE: Well yes, but it should have brought more than six dollars.

CLIFF: Actually, it brought twelve. But I paid off a couple of debts and I need something for the road, don't I?

FAYE: Sure, honey. *[Her eye strays unwillingly to the bag. She looks away and turns cold.]* I hope you paid the electric.

CLIFF: I did, yes. They're turning it back on tomorrow.

FAYE: *[Her eye is caught by the mirror. What she sees there distracts her.]* Cliff – do you think I look like Aunt Selma?

CLIFF: I suppose there is a family likeness. Why?

FAYE: Oh I don't know. It's just that … what's the point of fixing yourself up and taking care of yourself if you're destined to turn out like Selma anyway. Maybe you should sleep in the back room huh, honey? *[She's suddenly Shirley Temple.]* I have to get up awful early t'morra. Got to see the bad old welfare lady.

CLIFF: Yes, of course. You get your rest, sweetheart. Perhaps I'll look in on the boys before I bed down.

FAYE: Don't go waking them now.

CLIFF: No, no, I'll just look in on them. Goodbye, darling. *[Heads offstage]*

FAYE: So long.

[Once CLIFF is gone FAYE takes out the cases for a better look and starts shining up the silver backs of the brushes. There is a stirring behind her —a shadowy figure she can't quite make out, a figure that looks a bit like her husband.]

SHADOW: Pretty shabby, Faye.

FAYE: What? Who's there! *[She goes towards the voice but the figure is elusive.]*

SHADOW: Shabby thing to do.

FAYE: Cliff?

SHADOW: And the way you said goodbye to him. For someone you're not going to see again. No intimate moments. No last words.

FAYE: Is that you? Cliff? Quit horsing around!

SHADOW: You took his last dime, too.

FAYE: So what else am I supposed to do? *[Gathers up dressing case in a possessive manner.]* I thought I knew everything there was to know about you, Cliff, and all along you were holding out on me. This must be worth twenty bucks, at least. What is it, a family heirloom? Cliff?

SHADOW: Not Cliff. *[He steps partly out of the gloom.]*

FAYE: You *are* Cliff.

SHADOW: Am I like him?

FAYE: Yes. No. You're too … .

SHADOW: Perhaps I'm what you want Cliff to be.

FAYE: Cliff isn't capable of being anything. He's a magazine hero. Weak and spineless.

SHADOW: And not rich enough.

FAYE: He was rich when I married him. Or I thought he was. A nice fat cheque from the folks every month.

SHADOW: A remittance man.

FAYE: As soon as we got married, the cheques from home stopped. I wasn't good enough for them.

SHADOW: You thought when the babies came along they might soften. You had two in a row, real fast.

FAYE: They had money to burn. Town houses, country houses. Stables and yachts. Gold rimmed potties to pee in. And what do I end up with? A tarnished dressing case. Probably isn't their best, either. This is probably second or third best, in their eyes. A castoff. I should get a few dollars for it, though. It's all silver. *[She opens it. To her surprise there is something inside. She pulls out some crisp new notes.]* Where did this come from? Fifty dollars, for God's sake. Just tucked here into the lid. Where did it come from?

SHADOW: That was the deal, wasn't it?

FAYE: Deal?

SHADOW: You get the money. I get … a little of your time.

FAYE: I didn't make any deal. *[SHADOW shrugs, walks away.]* Wait! I didn't say no, did I? Let's start over. You're giving me fifty dollars? And … and you say you want a little of my time?

SHADOW: I want … *[He slips a white satiny wrap over her shoulders.]* … to tell you stories.

FAYE: *[She strokes the wrap in wonder.]* So, tell me a story.

[As SHADOW tells his story he removes exotic undergarments from his pockets and passes them suggestively to FAYE. Chemise, panties, silk stockings — all white.]

SHADOW: There was once a woman who was unsatisfied in her marriage. The trouble was, her husband had no imagination. He just couldn't give her what she wanted. What's more, he didn't seem to care. She tried to bring the matter up with him, make suggestions, but he never understood.

She brooded about it for a while. Then she decided to take matters into her own hands. She advertised. There were a lot of replies, two that interested her. The first was in his middle age. Rich. Elegant. Claimed to be a count.

The second said he was a seaman but looked more like a gangster. He wore a wide brimmed hat and a dark striped suit with wide shoulders.

FAYE: Which one did she choose?

SHADOW: Both of them. On Tuesdays she was picked up by the count's chauffeur and taken to his country estate where she was subjected to various expensive pleasures. Do I have to be explicit? *[FAYE shrugs.]* On Thursdays she rented a small room near the docks where she was brutalized by the ruffian in the dark suit. She outfitted herself according to the experience. Tuesdays, white silk and furs. Thursdays she squeezed herself into black, skin-tight dresses and tarty shoes. For a long time the arrangement was satisfactory. Even her husband noticed an improvement in her colour.

Then, out of the blue, the count said he wanted to see her more often. She gave him Fridays. And the gangster, though he'd never shown he was interested, insisted on more frequent meetings, and so she gave him Mondays.

One day the count demanded Thursdays as well. She said that her husband was at home on Thursdays and she couldn't leave the house. The count said nothing but the next Thursday he followed her to the hotel near the docks. He stormed into the cheap little room and challenged his rival to a duel.

FAYE: A duel? With swords and things?

SHADOW: Revolvers. The duel was to take place the following week in an open field on the edge of the city. That morning the woman rose before dawn and clothed herself in a clinging silk garment — the left side was white, the right black, like a harlequin. Her husband, suspicious of her strange actions, followed her to the field. She refused to speak to him.

A black limousine pulled up at one end of the field, at the other a white phaeton. The two assailants got out, faced each other and raised their revolvers.

The woman stood watching, no expression on her face. "I will kill the survivor," said her husband. But there was no need. Each was a deadly shot. Both were killed. The husband drove the woman home, where he stripped off her harlequin robe and forced her to confess the entire story. When she finished he led her from the room without speaking. From then on he was imaginative and masterful and as brutal as anyone could have wished. She never had reason to advertise again.

FAYE: Where did you get *that* one from?

SHADOW: Same place I got the money.

FAYE: Fifty bucks and a good story too. *[Brushes his cheek, all kittenish.]* It must have been some place.

SHADOW: It was.

FAYE: I'd offer you a drink but I'm stony. *[Looks at the money in her hand.]* Well I was until … .

SHADOW: *[With a flourish magically reveals a store of liquor.]* What would you like? Irish? Rye? *[He pours from a decanter into a heavy cut glass.]*

FAYE: This is real crystal! *[He adds some ice from a silver bucket.]* Chipped ice. My God, this is class, isn't it. Mud in your eye. Oh!

[She looks anxiously into the mirror.]

SHADOW: Something wrong?

FAYE: For a second there I could see Aunt Selma smirking at me.

SHADOW: For the last fifteen of her twenty-eight years, Faye has been obsessed with eradicating all traces of her family from her face …

FAYE: It's not just her face, it's that slumping way she walks. Why can't she walk upright like God meant her to. It drives me crazy!

SHADOW: … working hard remodelling herself to be like the women who beam out at her from magazines and film screens.

FAYE: If you saw her walk you'd know what I mean. Ankles streaming over the edges of her slippers. Breasts sagging down over her belt. If I turn out like that I'll kill myself! *[Spots the dressing case where some more bills are revealed.]* More money! Where does this come from?

SHADOW: I do things.

FAYE: Bad things, I suppose.

SHADOW: *[Smiles.]* Supposable things.

FAYE: And you just give this away. To people like me.

SHADOW: Like you.

FAYE: *[Suddenly a little worried.]* I'm not crazy about rye. I'm not crazy about … lots of things.

SHADOW: *[While she speaks he slips in a whispered word now and then.]* Supposable.

FAYE: What you have to understand about Cliff is how he brought all my dreams crashing down.

SHADOW: *Succulent.*

FAYE: I had him cast as the hero and almost from the first he was a disappointment. The minute things got tough the backbone went out of him. It was pathetic how fast he crumbled.

SHADOW: *Sinister.*

FAYE: At first I played the little woman who coped. I cleaned this place top to bottom every day, I washed the windows every week, every window in the goddamned house, which shows you how crazy I was.

SHADOW: You had a roof over your head.

FAYE: Some roof. Stuck between the river and the railway tracks. You can see St. George's Island from here. They have a zoo on the Island. I take the boys sometimes in the afternoons to see the animals.

Come and see this. *[Gestures him to the window.]* See what they're doing? Those constructions over there. You can just make them out. They're building huge plaster dinosaurs. The country knee-deep in depression and that's all they can do with their money.

[FAYE crosses to the other side of the room.]

FAYE: From this side of the house you can see the railway tracks. When a train goes by, Sandford and Benjy stand on the couch to watch. The train is always piled high with men — sitting, standing, lying on the tops of the cars, clinging to the sides — all heading west, looking for work. A few hours later another train goes by, heading east, swarming with men looking for work. If you saw it in a movie it would be funny.

SHADOW: You sent Cliff off to ride the cars.

FAYE: It was his decision.

SHADOW: It was cute the way you did it. Making him think it was his own idea.

FAYE: He had to, so we could get the welfare.

SHADOW: Taking his last dollar and his family keepsake. That was cute too. And nervy. You're one tough cookie.

FAYE: It wasn't stealing. I'm his wife. He wouldn't begrudge it.

[SHADOW smiles knowingly. This irritates FAYE.]

FAYE: Do you know what it's like living with a man like Cliff? Oh, he tries. Takes any work going. He works on city projects, planting trees, digging drainage ditches. But there's no purpose in anything he does.

SHADOW: *[Slipping a finger under the lapel of her wrap.]* Does white interest you? It interests me.

FAYE: He has no plan. Something comes up, he does it. Otherwise he sits around till something comes up.

SHADOW: Old white flesh, drained of blood.

FAYE: After a while it rubs off on you. That's the scary part. I don't want to drift like that. *[SHADOW still toys with her lapel. She grabs his hand, emphasizing her point.]*

SHADOW: White as snow. White as death.

FAYE: I don't want to go day after day on bread and potatoes with no heat, no electricity and barely enough clothes to stuff a busted window pane.

SHADOW: White as a baby's teeth.

FAYE: Not enough. Never enough! I don't want those words in my life!

SHADOW: White as a voyeur's prick.

[Pause.]

FAYE: It's too dark in here.

SHADOW: Faye wants light. Let there be light. *[He switches on a beautiful lamp.]*

FAYE: The electric's been cut off. Where did that come from?

SHADOW: You should know.

FAYE: I've never had a lamp like this.

SHADOW: Faye never remembers. She never wants to admit that all this is really her doing. The crystal. The perfumes. The dresses.

FAYE: Dresses?

[She discovers a hoard of dresses, different styles and textures, silks and feathers and sateens, some in bright colours, others suffused and demure.]

FAYE: I don't believe this! Linen, voile, silk. *[FAYE is distracted, delighted, overwhelmed with dresses. She holds them up to herself looking in the mirror.]* This is real silk. It was made for me.

SHADOW: Silk and fur and linen, each has its own texture, its own scent, its own story. *[He holds a beautiful white dress up to her.]*

FAYE: *[Holds the dress up to herself and looks in the mirror.]* Story?

SHADOW: I knew someone who was born when the white thorn was in bloom. The mother said it was bad luck. She wouldn't allow the flowers into the house. But a careless servant brought a bough of it into the room where the baby slept.

The child grew up to be a beautiful woman. But she was unable to speak. Not a word could she utter. It didn't seem to matter. She had many suitors, among them a king of great power. The king showered her with precious gifts and saw that she lacked for nothing. He offered her his kingdom and asked for her hand in marriage. The girl accepted him but, worried that she couldn't speak, sought the advice of a wise woman. "The solution is easy," said the wise women. "The reason you cannot speak is that a thorn from the white thorn tree is lodged behind your ear. Remove the thorn and you will no longer be dumb."

The girl was overjoyed and wanted the woman to remove it at once. The wise woman hesitated. "There is a drawback," she said. "If I remove the thorn you will be able to speak but your words will have such wisdom and power that you will no longer be the king's darling." The girl smiled and signalled to the woman to leave the thorn where it was.

[Pause.]

FAYE: She should have pulled the thorn.

SHADOW: She wouldn't have been his good and innocent darling any more.

FAYE: She could have faked it.

[SHADOW smiles and sips his drink.]

FAYE: Not much of a story.

SHADOW: The stories are for *my* satisfaction.

[FAYE fumbles through the shoes, trying and discarding them.]

FAYE: I planted a garden the first years of our marriage. The carrots were puny. The radishes went to wood. Something nipped off the beans as soon as they came out. Most of the time we lived on porridge and potatoes.

There was no money for fuel or boots. Sometimes Selma came to visit. She'd bring corn, fruitcake, cast-off clothing. She always pressed a dollar or two in my hand before she left. It wasn't for me. She never had any use for me and didn't pretend to. But there were the boys to think about. She couldn't let her own flesh and blood starve, could she? That's what she'd say.

[She finds a pair of shoes she likes and puts them on. She moves to the window.]

FAYE: Sometimes I feel I'm drifting with no shore in sight.

SHADOW: *[Echoes her, whispering.] Drifting.*

FAYE: *[Gesturing at the concrete dinosaurs.]* Look at those things. The moonlight makes them seem alive. Great beasts floating in the moonlight.

SHADOW: *Floating.*

FAYE: *[Sings in a soft, husky whisper.]* "I went to the animal fair. /The birds and the beasts were there. / The big baboon by the light of the moon/ was combing his auburn hair ... ." I'll take the boys there tomorrow. They like the zoo.

SHADOW: The boys? The boys aren't here. You know that.

FAYE: They're in their beds. *[Tries to read his face.]* You've done something to them! What have you done with them? *[She runs off.]* Sanford! Benjy!

SHADOW: *[Takes Faye's seat and opens a pot of powder. Sings in a broken, dead voice as he powders his face white.]*

> Take the face as a warning
> Red lips. White skin.
> White fringe of lashes
> The sudden Joker grin
> Vacant eyes
> The sudden Joker grin.
>
> Bloodless encounters
> You can never win
> Take the face as a warning
> Immaculate as sin

Leprous dreams
The sudden Joker grin.

[FAYE *comes back distracted, confused.*]

SHADOW: You put them in a home.

FAYE: Yes, I know. For a moment I ... . I visit them sometimes.

SHADOW: Once.

FAYE: It's not so bad. They get to play in the woods with the other boys. Build forts for cowboys and Indians. It's very nice. They make little fires under the trees and fry potatoes. They teach them how to darn socks there too and take care of themselves. It's better than I could do for them.

[SHADOW *hums his song and applies red lipstick.*]

FAYE: [*Finds more money in the case.*] This is so incredible. What do you do for this?

SHADOW: [*Hums on.*]

FAYE: You rob people, don't you.

SHADOW: [*Speaks.*] Red lips. White skin.

FAYE: You do awful things. I can tell.

SHADOW: Vacant eyes.

FAYE: Prostitution? Protection?

SHADOW: [*Whispers.*] The sudden Joker grin.

FAYE: Murder?

SHADOW: Not yet.

FAYE: Not yet. Then there's time.

SHADOW: I doubt it.

FAYE: What can I do?

SHADOW: You could give up the money.

FAYE: I would. But it keeps appearing.

SHADOW: Just stop spending it.

FAYE: Yes, I will.

SHADOW: Will you? You'll give up this voluptuous life I provide for you? The little package of bills every morning? I only ask for a few moment's warmth. *[He touches her cheek and she shrinks back.]*

FAYE: Don't!

SHADOW: Give it up then.

FAYE: I'll get a job. This guy I know at Woolworth's will hire me. He's as good as said.

SHADOW: If you say so.

FAYE: I'll throw it away. *[Flings case across room.]*

SHADOW: You've already tried that.

FAYE: *[Picks up case.]* Look at it. Is it any wonder it tempted me? I could see right away it was something special.

SHADOW: Something you could get a few bucks for.

FAYE: Something that would have special meaning for me. *[Traces the design on the leather.]* I feel like it's been with me forever.

SHADOW: *[Whispers an echo.] Ever ever ever ever ... .*

FAYE: I've tried selling it. But I can't. The leather is as soft as skin.

SHADOW: *Skin ...*

FAYE: It was well cared for at one time. Cream rubbed into it. *[Removes more money.]* I needed the money. But I can stop now.

SHADOW: There is a little maggot of independence in Faye.

FAYE: I'll just put it back. I'll put it in his bag where I found it.

SHADOW: His bag? Cliff left months ago.

FAYE: He's sleeping in the back room.

SHADOW: The boys weren't there, were they?

FAYE: This is just some stupid dream I'm having. He *is* there. *[She looks into the case.]* A letter. Addressed to me.

SHADOW: Already opened. Some time ago.

[FAYE, letter in hand, pours herself another drink. She reads silently while SHADOW says the words.]

SHADOW: My Darling Faye,

I've been everywhere you can name looking for work. There's not much going on in the way of jobs. I signed up with a harvesting outfit near Swift Current but we got hailed out in three counties. I've enclosed a little something … .

FAYE: Four lousy bucks.

SHADOW: I'll send you more when I can.

[FAYE throws the letter down, losing interest. SHADOW picks it up and moves closer to her as he recites the letter.]

SHADOW: I hear you gave up the boys.

FAYE: He must have been talking to Selma.

SHADOW: I'm sure you did it for the best. I'm sure you miss them badly. I know I do. And I miss you too. Especially you. I can't wait till we're together again. A thousand kisses. *[He strokes FAYE's neck.]*

FAYE: I don't like you touching me.

[SHADOW drops the letter and drifts off in a provocative manner. FAYE doesn't notice. She picks up the letter and goes on talking as though he's still there.]

FAYE: Cliff died a few days after he sent this, it must have been. It was a senseless, stupid death. Fell off the top of a car pulling out of Brandon … . Now I can never … .

SHADOW: *[Whispering offstage; at this point, FAYE cannot see him.]* Never … .

FAYE: Nothing can … .

SHADOW: *Nothing … .*

FAYE: Where does the money come from? What do you do for it?

SHADOW: Everything now. Everything you can name.

FAYE: But I'm giving it up. *[Distracted by her image in the mirror.]* Sometimes I think I'd like to be a dancer. A showgirl. Diamonds. Pearls. Lacquered hair. Everything glittering like the movies. I'm young. I still have my figure.

SHADOW: *Sugar …*

FAYE: Where are you!

SHADOW: *Sweet …*

FAYE: Where did you go?

SHADOW: *Nowhere …*

FAYE: *[Searching.]* Quit playing games. Show yourself.

SHADOW: I'm not really here. I'm just a notion in your mind.

FAYE: Stop it!

[SHADOW steps into the light. His face is chalk white with black smears, a mask-like apparition.]

SHADOW: Do I upset you? I'm really just an aspect of you.

FAYE: You don't look anything like me!

SHADOW: But I feel like you.

FAYE: No you don't!

[SHADOW moves towards her. FAYE backs off.]

FAYE: What do you want?

SHADOW: I want to dance. *[Reaches for her.]*

FAYE: Don't do that! Keep away! … .*[Moves out of reach.]* You're a ghost, aren't you.

SHADOW: Not a ghost.

FAYE: Then why am I so cold?

SHADOW: Warmth is a spiritual assumption. *[There is music and he moves slowly towards her.]* Join me.

FAYE: No!

SHADOW: We have been dancing together for a long time.

[As he tells his next story SHADOW dresses FAYE in a white gown and caresses her. At first she's mesmerized by her own loveliness, then the story wraps her round, possesses her.]

SHADOW: I will tell you the story of a woman who was very beautiful — not unlike yourself — white skin, dark hair. People ached to touch her. She kept herself from them, she kept herself for herself. The smooth silky skin, the creamy touch. She even avoided the caress of the sun. Not a freckle was allowed to mar that immaculate skin.

Some said it was what she ate, that she fed exclusively on red and white foods — apples, cream, rice, cherries. Others said that she bathed in milk and brandy. Still others said that the whiteness of her skin was bought at great cost from a sorcerer. "She can't be that white," they would say.

A great king wanted to marry her. She agreed, on one condition, that she be allowed to sleep alone. "Every evening I will come to your bed. But I will sleep in my own room." She was so beautiful the king could only agree. She was everything a king could desire in a consort. She was beautiful, lively, responsive to his every whim. She denied him nothing. But every evening before sleep took her she left his bed for her own. She slept alone in a chamber filled with lilies and snowdrops in a bed curtained with hangings of voile and white wool.

After a while the king came to regret his promise. In the dead of night a great restlessness would take possession of him and he would wander up and down the corridors of the palace. Invariably he would come to his queen's door but he could not enter as it was always bolted from the inside. He would stand in front of the door as though it were a puzzle to be solved. But it provided no solution. All was silent and still behind that door. And yet, if he put his ear to the door, there was a sound, a small spitting sound, like lard frying.

Every day the queen grew more beautiful. Every day the whispering and the rumours about the court grew more rabid. At last the king could no longer abide this mystery within his palace. One night he caused the chamber to be opened and the curtains of the bed to be drawn aside. There lay his queen, sleeping peacefully, as beautiful and as pale as alabaster. And lying beside her, entwining her body like a pale ropy vine, it's tongue forced deep into her mouth as she slept, was a great white snake.

FAYE: It's a dream, isn't it. A warning. Well I know it's been bad but it's not too late. I can get the boys back. I can … . It's all been a dream … .

SHADOW: Yes. How could I exist after all? I'm just a part of your imagination.

[SHADOW *moves closer to* FAYE. *Faint music of a waltz can be heard, lurid and fatal, as Shadow clasp her in his arms. Faye struggles to avoid his embrace.*]

SHADOW: Just a notion in your mind.

FAYE: I want to stop now.

SHADOW: The corrupt white notion of frailty … .

FAYE: No.

SHADOW: The corrupt white notion of innocence … .

FAYE: I can't!

SHADOW: The corrupt white notion of purity … .

FAYE: Please!

[FAYE *cannot resist.* SHADOW *forces her to dance.*]

SHADOW: We'll dance now. What could be sweeter? We'll dance and dance until we melt into each other. Then I will tell you the story of the white kiss. The long, white, melting, serpent kiss.

[FAYE, *locked in* SHADOW's *embrace, dances until the lights fade.*]

Tango Noir

"One of us is dreaming and one of us is going to die."

Tango Noir was first performed at the
Edmonton Fringe Festival, August 1988.

Marguerite / Colette [Scene Two]	Alexandria Patience
Colette [Scene One] /	Brian Jensen
Captain Bouchardon /	
Sister Maria / Henri	

Director	Brenda Anderson
Lighting Design	Sandi Somers
Artwork	Bruce Pashak
Costume Design	Lillian Messer
Choreography	Susan Laing
Tango and Soundscape	Kevin Labchuk
Stage Manager	Nancy Jo Cullen

Characters

This play is for two actors:

A woman who plays
MARGUERITE [the dream Mata Hari in Scene One]
and the real life COLETTE in Scene Two

And a man who plays
The dream COLETTE in Scene One,
CAPTAIN BOUCHARDON [Marguerite's jailer] in Scene
One, SISTER MARIA in Scene One, and HENRI [Colette's
husband Henri de Jouvenal] in Scene Two

Set: Colette's study. The set is semi-real. Real furniture fades off into painted scenery suggestive of *The Cabinet of Dr. Caligari.* The scenery includes painted portraits of Willy and of Colette dressed as Mata Hari. These are almost life-sized and, later in the final scene, will be turned to show sketchy portraits of Cheri, nude but for a woman's kimono and a strand of pearls; and, draped in the same kimono, an elderly nude Colette.

Time: October 1917, shortly before the execution of Marguerite Zelle at the Palais de Vincennes, Paris, for treason. Better known as Mata Hari, Zelle had once taken Paris by storm with her exotic dancing and, more recently, had been pursuing a successful, albeit stormy, career as a courtesan. In 1917 she was 41 years old.

The play takes place in the dream life of Colette, who would have been known to Marguerite as a novelist and actress. Colette too had tried her hand at exotic dancing in a style and in costumes remarkably similar to Mata Hari's. In 1917 she was 44, and was working as a wartime journalist.

~~~~~~

SCENE ONE

[Darkness. Opening bar of tango. As the following lines are spoken we become gradually aware of two figures clasped intensely together. The music and the voices disrupt each other until finally lights are dimly up.]

COLETTE: Be aware at all times of flesh.

[Another brutal, disrupted bar.]

MARGUERITE: Think of the flesh in Degas — pink, raw, unidealized.

COLETTE: Flesh is innocent. I am not ashamed of it.

MARGUERITE: Just beset by it.

[The couple are dancing the tango. It is not a pretty dance but basic, brutal and fateful. COLETTE is dressed as a man, slender, elegant, hair tied back, a patch over one eye. MARGUERITE is in prison garb — a black, calf-length dress. Her black shoes have solid two inch heels and straps that come up a bit on the ankle.

At first they seem to be a male/female couple. MARGUERITE is a woman of a certain age, who moves with the grace of one who knows she is admired. COLETTE is energetic, dangerous, somewhat overwhelming in a male way. As they dance in the shadows their mood is brooding and tense. It is a moment of desire, dangerously intimate.]

MARGUERITE: *[Petulant, a woman who is in the presence of a dominating but indulgent lover]* I don't like this dance, Vadim.

COLETTE: I do. I like the meaty feel of it.

MARGUERITE: It's too raw. Besides, isn't the tango forbidden these days?

COLETTE: In dreams is anything forbidden?

MARGUERITE: Vadim. You're such a little tease. No! No more!

COLETTE: *[Holding her closer.]* It's like Kokoscha — violent, disembowelling.

MARGUERITE: Let go, Vadim. I mean it! *[Pushes him off.]* Damn! You've crushed my violets. Get me a drink, you clumsy brat. A glass of that lunel. And a cigarette.

[Her partner brings the wine and gives her a cigarette. The flare of the match illuminates his eye patch and reveals an enigmatic, androgynous face that is heavily powdered with a reddened rosebud mouth.]

MARGUERITE: *[Backing away in revulsion.]* You're not Vadim. *[Pulls off the patch.]* How dare you! You're not even .... *[She pulls away the ribbon that has tied the hair of her partner at the nape.]* Colette! What is this? What are you doing here? Why are you dressed as a man?

COLETTE: It could just as easily be the other way around.

MARGUERITE: No it couldn't. I could never. Keep away! I thought you were Vadim.

COLETTE: Your baby lover?

MARGUERITE: I haven't seen him for so long. I don't even know what he's thinking these days. I don't even know if he's alive.

COLETTE: Here, drink your wine. And your cigarette's gone out. *[Hands the glass to MARGUERITE and gets out the matches. He strikes the match and lights her up. MARGUERITE takes a long, nicotine-starved drag.]*

MARGUERITE: My God, Colette! You looked just like him! You even sounded like him. What are you up to?

COLETTE: *[Sits down beside her, a little too close for MARGUERITE's comfort.]* Let's just say I like the tango.

MARGUERITE: Is this a dream?

COLETTE: Yes.

MARGUERITE: I thought so. Yes. It just has to be. Everything is so upended and absurd. My dreams are always a little bit absurd.

COLETTE: But it's not your dream, *cherie*. It's mine.

MARGUERITE: Why would I be in your dream?

COLETTE: Because you have something I want, Marguerite.

MARGUERITE: What?

COLETTE: Prison has been rough on you, Marguerite. You've aged.

MARGUERITE: Not that much, surely.

COLETTE: Eight months away from the embrace of your little Vadim. Look at your nails. Your hair. And your flesh. You've gone puffy. Like a corpse in water.

MARGUERITE: If you knew how I craved water. Gallons and gallons of hot, soapy water, scented with cologne. This *must* be your dream. Mine would have a tub in it, filled to the brim.

COLETTE: Like a corpse in water, Marguerite.

MARGUERITE: I'm at a disadvantage in this light. And without makeup — well, who wouldn't look like a corpse.

COLETTE: You always did have bad skin, though.

MARGUERITE: Nonsense. I've always had perfect skin. What are you doing! [COLETTE *has slipped a hand behind* MARGUERITE's *neck.*]

COLETTE: Why don't we say ... I'm reclaiming what's mine.

MARGUERITE: I don't understand.

COLETTE: Don't lie to me, Marguerite. I know what's mine when I see it. Willy was clever but I'm clever too. I've rooted out all his little *collaborateurs*. [*Plays with the hair at the nape of* MARGUERITE's *neck in a threatening way.*]

MARGUERITE: I never knew Willy!

COLETTE: My first husband ... . Shall I tell you what I was like once, Marguerite? I was an innocent little savage. I thought when you married someone you would be the sole object of his love. But with Willy I was never the only one. I was always one of a pair.

MARGUERITE: But that's why men have two arms, darling, to have a woman on each. The wife with her jewels and dresses, the mistress with *her* jewels and dresses, but always in two separate spheres.

COLETTE: Willy brought his conquests home.

MARGUERITE: Home? Surely not!

COLETTE: Was your double never made to dress like you? Wear her hair like you? Did she never sit across from you, a darker, more subtle twin of yourself?

MARGUERITE: Only in my fantasies. Or at the opera on occasion. Besides, in most cases *I* was the double.

COLETTE: I know.

MARGUERITE: But never yours, Colette, I promise you.

COLETTE: I always had this feeling with Willy's women that he was giving them something of mine. They'd smile at themselves in my mirror. Roll around in my bed. Call out to the birds from my window, and when they left I always had this suspicion that they'd gone off with something that belonged to me.

MARGUERITE: They'd probably gone off with a ten franc note from the housekeeping.

COLETTE: Willy gave out little bits of me like gifts, quite indiscriminately. I used to torture myself about it. Later I realized the best way was to be unemotional and deliberate. Now every time I find one of his women I embrace them. I draw them to me and make them give up what is mine.

[COLETTE *slips an arm about* MARGUERITE.]

MARGUERITE: Don't!

COLETTE: I make them give up what is mine and then I dispose of them.

MARGUERITE: What's that supposed to mean?

COLETTE: It means I'm here to supervise your death, Marguerite.

MARGUERITE: Ridiculous! Besides this is only a dream, remember?

COLETTE: One of us is dreaming and one of us is going to die.

MARGUERITE: But I was never one of Willy's women. I was only involved with important men.

COLETTE: Important! Willy dominated the entire cultural life of Paris!

MARGUERITE: The Bohemian cultural life. My lovers were all well connected. And rich. Willy could never have afforded the sort of life I expected.

[Momentarily losing interest in MARGUERITE, COLETTE *removes her jacket, exchanging it for a military tunic complete with ribbons and medals.]*

MARGUERITE: *[Adjusting the violets in her bosom]* Besides, he was so ugly! I saw him once or twice at Maxim's and the Brasserie, but I must say I could never understand his appeal. *[She spots the portrait of him.]* I mean look at him, paunchy, balding ... .

COLETTE: But you have to admit, distinguished. In bearing somewhat like England's Edward the Seventh, I always thought.

MARGUERITE: *[Studying the likeness.]* More like Queen Victoria. He would have looked terrible in a uniform. *[Noticing* COLETTE'*s jacket,* MARGUERITE *is suddenly aware of* COLETTE *in a new and more compelling light.]* My husband now ...

COLETTE: *[Consulting a notebook on the desk.]* That would be John Rudolph Macleod.

MARGUERITE: *Captain* Macleod. He put an advertisement in the Amsterdam News for a wife, if you can believe such a thing. "Captain in the Army of the Indies seeks a wife with a character to his taste." To his taste. Hah! I was an adolescent fool. We met in the foyer of the Rijksmuseum. He was fat, bald, suffered from at least three tropical diseases, and was crippled with a leg injury. He was also foul tempered, besotted with drink, and more than twice my age, and all I could see was his uniform. *[She has come gradually closer to* COLETTE *and is now playing with the brass buttons of the jacket.]*

[As MARGUERITE *speaks,* COLETTE *does up her tunic, tucks her trousers into her boots, clasps the belt, puts on a kepi, then strides about slapping her boots occasionally with a silver topped swagger stick. The light brightens, hardens. She is now Captain Bouchardon, a French security officer and Marguerite's jailer. Until now he's been sensually dangerous. Now he looks legally dangerous.]*

MARGUERITE: The regrettable fact is, I'm addicted to uniforms. Especially when I'm distressed. The weeks before my arrest I couldn't get enough of them.

COLETTE/BOUCHARDON: Yes. This extraordinary appetite for military men did not pass unnoticed by our observers. *[Consulting his file.]* January 9th: you were visited by a French aviator. January 10th, an ardent Sub-lieutenant came to your rooms. On the 12th it was "lunch" with a Lieutenant-colonel. You must have had one almost every day.

MARGUERITE: Sometimes two a day. Your observers were less than competent. It wasn't that hard to give them the slip.

COLETTE/BOUCHARDON: They were observant enough, Madame. How many officers does one have to entertain to fall under suspicion?

MARGUERITE: It is the war, after all, *Capitaine*. Officers are much more common in Paris than bankers. But even so I'd always choose an officer over a banker, or over anyone, for that matter. *[Toys with* BOUCHARDON'S *brass buttons.]* There's something different about a soldier. His destiny is uncertain. You meet with him and it might be the first of many times, it might be the last. He's significant in a way a banker can never be.

*[*COLETTE/BOUCHARDON *pushes her away in no uncertain terms and attends to the papers on his desk.]*

MARGUERITE: A uniform usually shows a man is prepared to do something about the world besides riffling through stacks of paper.

COLETTE/BOUCHARDON: This stack of papers, Madame, holds information vital to your well-being.

MARGUERITE: Ah yes. The daring aviator. The ardent Sub-lieutenant. And my pretty little Lieutenant-colonel. All closely questioned, I'm sure.

COLETTE/BOUCHARDON: We questioned them all, yes.

MARGUERITE: I can just picture it. *[Leaning over* COLETTE *as if interrogating him.]* Describe to me, my little Lieutenant-colonel, the exact nature of your activities with Madame Zelle, also known as Mata Hari. Ah, *lunch*. At the Café de Paris. Hmm, elegant. And then? Excuse me if I seem indelicate but it is vital to the security of France that you tell us. Her rooms! Now tell me. In her rooms did Madame *reveal* anything to you? I mean of a military nature.

COLETTE/BOUCHARDON: You should have been a lawyer. It is clear that your talents have been wasted, Madame.

MARGUERITE: Not entirely wasted. But tell me, *Capitaine*, what did your interrogation of these uniforms reveal about me? You did ask if I had encouraged discussions of military consequence, did you not?

COLETTE/BOUCHARDON: I did.

MARGUERITE: And?

COLETTE/BOUCHARDON: Invariably the answer was that you had not.

MARGUERITE: So why am I here?

COLETTE/BOUCHARDON: You are here, Madame, because France has need of you.

MARGUERITE: Well exactly. Exactly what I told that superior of yours, that imbecile Ladoux. But the man has no imagination. I offered my services and he had no idea how to use me. "I will go to the Germans," I said. "With my connections and my abilities, I can get right to the top."

COLETTE/BOUCHARDON: You think the Prussians and the Austrians are just waiting to receive you?

MARGUERITE: I'm talking about the Crown Prince and his

brother. I lived for two years in Berlin with my lover Keipert. A delicious man. In bed he was rough as hell but he was generous. For two years I lived in wonderful luxury. I got to know Berlin society very well, let me tell you. Keipert was well-connected and liberal in his introductions That was how I got to know the Crown Prince.

COLETTE/BOUCHARDON: This gets more and more like one of your fairy tales, Madame. You can't just dream up a costume and a scenario and dance your way into the bedroom of the German royal family.

MARGUERITE: Ladoux is going to give me a million francs to do just that.

COLETTE/BOUCHARDON: A million francs? Impossible!

MARGUERITE: That was the agreement. Why should I do it for less? And I've already proven what I can do. If you look through that file of yours you'll find I sent no fewer than five very important communications to M'sieur Ladoux.

[COLETTE/BOUCHARDON *ignores her and shuffles through his papers.*]

MARGUERITE: Aren't they there? I can enumerate them. First there were the submarine landings in French Morocco. Did you read that? And then … you aren't listening to me.

COLETTE/BOUCHARDON: It is pointless to tire yourself, Madame. The role of heroine is not what we have in mind for you.

MARGUERITE: Oh? And what role did you have in mind?

COLETTE/BOUCHARDON: It is the one you play so well. The one the public is familiar with and is always hungry for.

MARGUERITE: Mata Hari? She was a pre-war creature. Not the kind the public is all that interested in these days.

COLETTE/BOUCHARDON: I think the public is very interested in that sort of woman right now. Someone who can epitomize the evils of the war. Someone who can take on all the guilt and animosity. Mata Hari. Destroyer of men.

MARGUERITE: Don't talk like that. I'm not like that. I've never been like that. You can't make me a scapegoat. You can't prove a thing against me.

COLETTE/BOUCHARDON: No? *[Picking up a page.]* The British it seems have suspected you for some time of clandestine activities.

MARGUERITE: Suspicion is not evidence.

COLETTE/BOUCHARDON: They detained you, last December I believe, at the port of Falmouth.

MARGUERITE: They mistook me for someone else.

COLETTE/BOUCHARDON: A Clara Benedix.

MARGUERITE: Clara. Marta. It was something like that.

COLETTE/BOUCHARDON: A known German spy. And why did they take you for this Benedix woman?

MARGUERITE: They suspect everyone of a colourful character. They had a picture of her in Spanish costume. Even a casual observer could see it wasn't me. But they insisted on going through the motions. They tore my cabin apart, removed the mirror from the wall, they interrogated me for three days. All those questions and I didn't have a thing to tell them.

COLETTE/BOUCHARDON: *[Picks up another page.]* The statement of Berthe Boucher, manicurist at the Plaza.

MARGUERITE: She did my nails three or four times.

COLETTE/BOUCHARDON: She claims that you called the British imbeciles.

MARGUERITE: They've never given me cause to think otherwise.

COLETTE/BOUCHARDON: You also said that the Belgians were a filthy race.

MARGUERITE: Now that she made up. I've always found the Belgians to be very clean. In fact Colonel Beaufort, no doubt he's on your list there, makes a point of bathing before and after.

COLETTE/BOUCHARDON: Before and after what?

MARGUERITE: Everything, darling.

COLETTE/BOUCHARDON: Mlle Boucher also claims that when you read of the 200,000 dead at Verdun, you laughed aloud.

MARGUERITE: Ridiculous. Why should I do such a thing. The woman is a sensationalist. So far your scraps of evidence are just so much sugar in the rain. You'd better have something more incriminating than this if you hope to bring me to trial.

COLETTE/BOUCHARDON: Perhaps we have, Madame. *[Picks up a cosmetic case and empties its contents on the desk.]*

MARGUERITE: My toiletry bag! If you knew how I've missed it.

COLETTE/BOUCHARDON: Please, Madame! *[Fends her off.]* Perhaps you would like to explain the contents of this case.

[He holds up one item at a time.]

MARGUERITE: Goodness, I'd have thought anyone would know.

COLETTE/BOUCHARDON: Please, Madame.

MARGUERITE: Well, that's face powder.

And that is pomade for the hair. To keep it smooth and bring out all its natural lustre.

Soap of course.

Lip rouge.

Kohl.

COLETTE/BOUCHARDON: Kohl?

MARGUERITE: Antimony. It heightens the colour of the eyes. *[Moves closer.]* And here you have madder for reddening the gums. It makes the teeth appear whiter. Those are my perfumes. Chypre, patchouli, jasmine. I've always been able to wear the exotic fragrances. I've missed them so much.

[Again he warns her off.]

COLETTE/BOUCHARDON: And these?

MARGUERITE: Those are just pharmaceuticals: headache powders, stomach lozenges, peppermint. Hydrogen peroxide for whitening the little hairs over the lip. Well, *Capitaine*. Now I have revealed all my secrets.

COLETTE/BOUCHARDON: Not quite all. There remain two small bottles.

MARGUERITE: Oh?

COLETTE/BOUCHARDON: This, from Robert & Co., 5 rue de la Paix, based on the prescription of a Dr. Verne. Our chemists have analyzed it and found it to be composed of one part bi-iodure de mercure, seven parts iodure de potassium and one hundred parts water

MARGUERITE: I had no idea!

COLETTE/BOUCHARDON: And the second seems to be of Spanish origin, a bottle of pills composed of oxycyanure de mercure.

MARGUERITE: What point are you trying to make?

COLETTE/BOUCHARDON: Our chemists have discovered that if the contents of this bottle were mixed with forty to fifty times its volume of water, and if these pills were dissolved in five hundred times their volume of water, both would make excellent invisible inks.

MARGUERITE: Really. How novel. I didn't realize that spermicides were so versatile.

COLETTE/BOUCHARDON: I beg your pardon. You called them … ?

MARGUERITE: Spermicides, M'sieur. Dissolved in the amounts of water you indicated they both make excellent antiseptics. You will probably find a bottle of one or the other within hand's reach of most bidets in Paris.

[The captain throws the bottle across the room. MARGUERITE laughs.]

MARGUERITE: I have a feeling that Captain Bouchardon won't be raising the matter of secret inks at my trial.

COLETTE/BOUCHARDON: Captain Bouchardon doesn't need to. There will be evidence enough. *[Rips off his belt angrily and unbuttons his tunic.]*

MARGUERITE: Oh God, let me at these treasures.

[The light softens, warms. MARGUERITE, now free to use the cosmetics, kneels with the case in front of her and begins to make up her face. The Captain, COLETTE once more, removes his tunic and kneels beside her.]

COLETTE: And now, Marguerite performs the time honoured rituals on her poor ravaged face. For the bruised soul there is no better remedy than the soothing alchemy of the fat powder puff, the blackened brush.

[As he talks, COLETTE imitates MARGUERITE's makeup ritual. At times they help each other. The mood is companionable, gentle, dreamy and sad.]

COLETTE: First the velvety layer of powder, smoothing away the creases and shadows until a clear, kitteny triangle glows back in the mirror.

Then, to enhance the spirit and banish pallor, a pink smear on each cheek.

Next she blackens the lashes, double blacks them and applies a rim of kohl, top and bottom. Her eyes come out from behind the dullness that clouds them and shine in the old way, luminous and deep. Her face is not without real beauty at this moment.

Marguerite devised this little mask for herself twenty years ago. She didn't need it then, of course. But it is what most of us do. If you start out with it early it becomes your true face and there is nothing to change or add to when there is something to disguise.

[COLETTE rises, puts on an elegant kimono and draws it close, gracefully absorbed, as in a reverie. MARGUERITE gathers up the cosmetics.]

MARGUERITE: Tell me about Willy.

COLETTE: What's to tell?

MARGUERITE: He wasn't all that bad, was he? There must have been some advantages.

COLETTE: Were there advantages with Captain Macleod?

MARGUERITE: Rudy? No. He gave me children, of course, but one died and the other ... he took her away from me. Willy at least gave you fame.

COLETTE: Oh, yes. Like a circus monkey has fame. But he did make a writer of me.

MARGUERITE: Is it true that Willy locked you in your room?

COLETTE: Every day without fail. And he kept me there till I'd done the required number of pages. When you think about it! But you know, it never would have occurred to me on my own that I could be a writer. And there I was, churning out best sellers as though it were the most natural thing in the world, just because Willy told me to. It may have seemed like torture at the time but it wasn't the worst thing he did to me. It was the disillusionment I couldn't forgive. To find my debonair prince of culture was really a toad.

MARGUERITE: You don't have to tell me. You turn in your marriage bed one night and find you've attached yourself not to a hero, as you had imagined, but an old woman — no, someone with no sex at all. Fat and frightened. Just a frightened old fool.

COLETTE: And you live in fear that he will find out that you know. Somehow that was the worst thing for me. Knowing that neither of us could handle his inadequacies.

MARGUERITE: You know, you could take this picture of Willy, put a uniform on him and an extra chin or two and you'd have Rudy. To think I stayed with him for eight years.

COLETTE: The miracle is not that you stay for so long but that you ever break away.

MARGUERITE: Well I did, and I count that as one of my great achievements.

COLETTE: But what did you escape to after all, Marguerite?

MARGUERITE: Fame and fortune and a wonderful career.

COLETTE: Wonderful?

MARGUERITE: I made 135 appearances that first year.

COLL: Yes, I remember. One couldn't go anywhere that year without stumbling over you.

MARGUERITE: Everybody wanted me. The Rothschilds. Madame Ducharme, Natalie Barney … .

COLETTE: God, I remember Natalie's affair. Weren't you on a horse or something? Those salons! Everyone kneeling at the altar of art, ready to be taken in by any little *artiste* that could find the price of a tinsel and paste brassiere.

MARGUERITE: My jewels were always authentic. Even my horse had turquoise studs in his trappings.

COLETTE: The horse deserved them. He was a thoroughbred.

MARGUERITE: It was an effective entrance, wasn't it? I've always been a superb equestrienne. But it was my dancing they were there to see.

COLETTE: I wouldn't have called it dancing, exactly.

MARGUERITE: As I recall, you were one of the most ardent imitators of my style.

COLETTE: *Your* style!

MARGUERITE: I invented it. The style and the role.

COLETTE: The role was there ready and waiting, my dear Marguerite. A little heap of scarves waiting to be stepped into. The public was thirsty for the fatal woman. You came along with all the faux mystique of those years in Java. Mata Hari the temptress, the all-consuming woman.

MARGUERITE: I invented myself. I brought the mystery of the east to Paris.

COLETTE: It didn't matter that the mythology was mixed up – the role caught fire and that was enough. All you had to do was maintain a certain grace and hope that the scrutiny didn't go too deep.

MARGUERITE: The public were obsessed with me. For them I *was* Mata Hari.

COLETTE: It was their own idea of the destroyer they were seeing. You were a fleeting image on the wall, like one of those Javanese shadow puppets in the Guimet Museum.

MARGUERITE: You can be critical. And yet you spent, how many years was it, trying to give the public what it wanted.

COLETTE: It was different with me.

MARGUERITE: Really. *[Refers to the portrait.]* A picture of you? If you showed this to most people they would think it was me. The tiara, the jewelled harness, the flimsy veils. You've even got my pose!

COLETTE: I was never trapped in it the way you were. For you the role was everything. I was never interested in the role. It was the backstage life, the women wilting in their dressing rooms, covering up their tired faces with makeup, clinging to their slender boy/men, washing out their stockings in the sink.

MARGUERITE: But playing to the crowd. Don't tell me you didn't find that exciting.

COLETTE: Perhaps. God knows, I did it for long enough. But to tell you the truth, what remains for me was on the other side of the curtain. The showgirls with their little cat faces and brutal little ankles. Their bitten nails and dyed hair. Just a bunch of grubby girls playing dress-up. Give her some feathers and rhinestones and some sequins and black silk and anyone can look interesting. I still miss the company of those sleazy little queens and I'm still hungry for that particular backstage smell. Powder and cheap perfume and sweat.

MARGUERITE: Lord! You're starting to sound like one of your books. I've tried reading them. They're not to my taste. Who wants to read about makeup and cats and fading lovers and dreary little rooms with no water?

COLETTE: Those who understand the magic of real things.

MARGUERITE: There's too much sweat in your books. All the smells and the noise and the shrubbery growing up around you as you read. The sand blowing over everything. The stink of fish on your hands, the smell of salt and pollen and armpits. I always feel I need a bath after one of your stories.

COLETTE: I expect you need a bath after most of the things you do.

MARGUERITE: Go ahead. Take pleasure in your little malices. And yet, Colette, consider why I am here.

COLETTE: You are here to be disposed of.

MARGUERITE: Didn't you say there was something of mine you wanted?

COLETTE: Did I?

MARGUERITE: Maybe I stand for something that has more of a hold on you than you're willing to admit.

COLETTE: Hardly.

MARGUERITE: The desire to bring the world to its knees, as I did. The desire to make men do what you wish, the way I did. To be the jailor.

COLETTE: It is not my goal in life to hold men captive. Not in the way you do. Extorting money for an hour with your body. Playing instructress to teenaged boys!

MARGUERITE: Vadim is twenty-five years old.

COLETTE: And you?

MARGUERITE: Younger than you. Vadim says I don't look a day over thirty.

COLETTE: They're looking for mothers, you know. All those young wounded men.

MARGUERITE: Vadim wanted me before he was wounded.

COLETTE: Lucky for you it was the eye. *[Slips the eyepatch back on.]* What was it, shrapnel? One eye less to see you with, my dear?

MARGUERITE: Don't!

COLETTE: Do I look like him now?

MARGUERITE: No. Vadim is young. His body is honey coloured, and young. His hair is golden, like those little English biscuits you have with sherry. And young. And the fragrance of him, in his hair, behind his ears, I'm addicted to that smell. It's like honey and wine. And young.

COLETTE: And you, Marguerite, are no longer young. He may say you look thirty but each day the lie is larger in his mouth. You live in fear that he will turn round one day and see you for the hag you are.

MARGUERITE: You sound as though you have a stake in that fear.

COLETTE: I have a stake in all the fears of women. Young men looking better and better to us. The struggle of the maternal and sexual in one heartbeat. Mother and son. Mother and daughter. Lover and lover. *[Pulls MARGUERITE close.]* It's all a joke, Marguerite. The lust of the old. The wide-open eyes of the young.

MARGUERITE: You French! Why must you always be so complicated!

COLETTE: I just like to woo things, extract the most from their existence. To crush violets, for example *[Mischievously takes the violets from MARGUERITE's bosom.]* and devour them.

MARGUERITE: I don't think you take enough baths, Colette.

COLETTE: Sometimes I feel … I want to devour everything. Leaves, flowers, the pollen in the air, the honey in the wind.

MARGUERITE: Stop it!

COLETTE: I'll devour you and write a book about it. Or I'll write the book first. I often have to write about things before I can experience them. I could write a book about loving young men. And then I might become a lover of young men.

Perhaps that is what I want from you, Marguerite. The thirst for young men.

MARGUERITE: It's the first, the very first time I've been in love. Oh I've had fun with men. I've known lust, passion, and long term friendship. Old Clunet, my lawyer, has been devoted to me since I first came to Paris. And my oldest friend, Marguerie, still cares for me. But Vadim. I spend all my waking hours plotting how to be with him or plotting how to make him happy. *[COLETTE takes her hand and examines it.]* A million francs, Colette. Think what I could do for Vadim with a million francs.

COLETTE: *[Holding MARGUERITE's hand palm up.]* You will never collect it, my petite.

MARGUERITE: Don't!

COLETTE: *[Puts the violets back in MARGUERITE's bosom.]* Poor Marguerite. We're not so different, after all. Both lured into marriages of disillusionment. Both used by men. Both moulded by men. Both despised by our daughters.

MARGUERITE: I am not despised by my daughter! My daughter *loves* me.

COLETTE: Both adored by our daughters, then.

MARGUERITE: My old servant Annie once wrote to me that Non, that's my daughter's name, my little Non carries her lunch to school in a biscuit tin with a picture of Mata Hari on it. I don't know why that tale gives me such ridiculous satisfaction. Annie probably made it up to please me.

COLETTE: There, you see? We both have devoted companions named Annie. We both love biscuit tins with Mata Hari on them and we are both incredibly spendthrift. Everything you earn goes on clothes and jewels.

MARGUERITE: And Vadim.

COLETTE: Mine goes on garlic and gardens and oceans of blue paper.

[COLETTE goes to the desk and turns on the lamp. It lights up a pile of blue paper lying there.]

COLETTE: Of all the appetites I have, the one for paper is the most powerful and the one easiest to satisfy. It is not so easy to create the conditions for consuming it. The arrangement for the light. The filling of the pens. The balance of the desk. I am more careful in my arrangements for the use of paper than I am for the accommodation of a lover.

MARGUERITE: Paper is the one commodity my jailors are ungrudging of, no doubt hoping I will forget myself one day and cover the pages they give me with confessions. I've probably been using as much of this lately as you. What else is there to do in prison but write letters. Letters to Vadim, to my little Non, to Marguerie and to that bastard Bouchardon.

[MARGUERITE takes a sheet of paper and begins a frenzy of letter writing that is not so much informative as indicative of her desperation and need to communicate.]

MARGUERITE: My Dear Captain Bouchardon,

When, when, when are you going to do something about these unspeakable conditions. I need water, soap, food that is at least edible — and couldn't you see your way to letting me have a picture of Vadim? At what possible risk could it put France to allow me one small photograph!

[Takes new sheet of paper.]

Darling Vadim,

I can't imagine why I have not heard from you. Are you taking care of yourself? Eating well? I have asked Clunet to send you some money. I long to see you, to cover you with kisses.

[Another sheet of paper.]

My Dear Captain,

Please be so good as to have my clothes picked up from my dressmaker Madame Bergeron of 15 Rue de Princes. Regarding my statement of the fifteenth …

[Another sheet]

My Dear Captain,

Once again I will try to explain myself. Regarding the suspicions of the British, I can only say …

[Another sheet]

My Dear Bouchardon,

Concerning the communications sent to Colonel Ladoux from Madrid, it must be realized that …

[Another sheet]

How long must I languish in this rat-infested hole? If you could only experience it, the lice, the wretched little window, the damp walls. No communication with anyone, Vadim, my daughter, my friends. Are you sending *any* of the letters I write?

[Another sheet]

Are you paying any attention at all to my letters? You have not answered one. I spend my days in explanations, in reviewing and reviewing *ad nauseum* the facts in the case. If you would do likewise you would have to find me innocent of all charges …

[New sheet of paper]

My dear Captain,

I beseech you from the depths of my despair …

[New sheet of paper]

My dear Vadim …

[Takes new sheet of paper. Her writing grows more and more furious.]

My Dearest Non,

Annie tells me …

[New sheet of paper]

Vadim, my beloved …

[New sheet of paper]

Vadim …

[New sheet of paper]

Vadim …

COLETTE: Vadim, Vadim, Vadim! *[Snatches away the pen.]*

MARGUERITE: Vadim smells of pennies and chocolate and he has the hands of an angel. If only they would give me his letters. If only I could see him. I live for the day we are reunited.

COLETTE: It won't happen. It will never happen.

MARGUERITE: How can you know that!

COLETTE: *[Takes her hand.]* It's here in your hand. You will not leave St. Lazarre till the day of your death.

MARGUERITE: *[Pulls away her hand with a small cry of protest.]*

COLETTE: They will arrive for you. Bouchardon, the nuns, the examining magistrates and others. Nine of them in all. Sister Leonide will turn up the gaslight and gently pray over you.

MARGUERITE: It is not possible.

COLETTE: The two who share your cell will be sent away. The thief and the prostitute who murdered her baby. They were only brought in to discourage you from suicide. Their usefulness is over. You will appeal to Clunet.

MARGUERITE: My lawyer, he will be there? Dear old Clunet.

COLETTE: Faithful to the end. You will appeal to him and he will break down in tears. He will tell you: "My dear lady, your request for clemency has been rejected."

MARGUERITE: It's not possible. Not possible.

COLETTE: The younger nun …

MARGUERITE: Sister Maria … *[She is now moving into the reality of her death.]*

COLETTE: … will also cry.

MARGUERITE: Don't be afraid, Sister. I shall know how to die. Come, you will have to help me with my corset.

COLETTE: [As Sister Maria] I will ask them to wait in the corridor if you wish.

MARGUERITE: [Dressing may be mimed or real.] This isn't the moment to be prudish, Sister. I always liked this dress. [Takes up a pearl grey dress.] The colour is both demure and tempting, like a dove's breast. Nuns should wear this colour. I'll leave it to you, shall I? There! What do you think? Wide skirts are so flattering. I always think you can face anything if you're dressed for it. Oh, and my violets. They've done me for eight months — they can perform one more time.

[Standing before the mirror, she adjusts the front of her dress and resettles the violets in the nest of her bosom. Finally satisfied, she looks coquettishly at herself, then picks up stockings and slips them over her hand.]

MARGUERITE: Yes, these are real silk. Imagine, Sister, silk stockings in the war! A miracle? No. My old Clunet came through for me.

And now the hat. [She takes down a felt tricorn hat.] It just isn't right. It needs a veil. I know, I know. No hatpins allowed. [Takes shoes from a paper-lined box.] I bought these on a whim last autumn. The most expensive shoes I've ever owned. Look at the workmanship. The stitching, the patina. These shoes are a great satisfaction to me, Sister Maria.

COLETTE/SISTER MARIA: In Burgundy they have a saying about the dead: "Be sure to dress them in new shoes so they will have no excuse to return."

MARGUERITE: You don't need to worry about me, Sister. Now, what about my coat? Will I need it? What is the weather like? [She draws long gloves on and buttons them.]

COLETTE/SISTER MARIA: It is wet and there is a chill in the air. You will need it. [Drapes a blue coat around MARGUERITE's shoulders.]

MARGUERITE: I have written letters. To my daughter. To Vadim and to Robert Marguerie. Give them to Clunet. He won't fail me.

COLETTE: *[Colette again]* They will never reach their destination.

MARGUERITE: Well. I am ready. Oh yes. Tell me. *[Hesitates and tries to keep the plea from her voice.]* Was there anything worth … in my life, you know … anything … ?

COLETTE: Yes. There was.

MARGUERITE: And will you write about it? For the world to know?

COLETTE: It won't matter to the world. It is of value only to me. A way of moving that's authentic. A sensuality of spirit. A dizzy submission to passion. A ridiculously inflated sense of self worth. There needs to be more of that, you know.

MARGUERITE: I'm glad there was something, after all.

[COLETTE in manner slips back into the role of Bouchardon.]

MARGUERITE: I want to die well.

COLETTE: You will be driven in a five-car contingent to the Palais de Vincennes. There the gates will close behind you and the cars will move across the cobblestones of the courtyard to the Caponierre. The field is broad and hummocky. Three hand-picked units of men will be waiting.

Sabre Main!

Presentez armes!

MARGUERITE: I don't think it would be good for your health to accompany me further.

[COLETTE takes out the blindfold.]

MARGUERITE: No. I don't want to be blindfolded or tied. Wait, though. How can I die if this is a dream? Can one really dream one's own death?

COLETTE: *[Coldly]* This is my dream, not yours.

MARGUERITE: In that case, why can't you … ?

COLETTE: Your firing squad will be composed of the youngest, choicest men from the front. You will blow a kiss to them.

MARGUERITE: I don't feel like blowing them a kiss.

COLETTE: You will blow a kiss to them.

MARGUERITE: *[Reluctantly blows a kiss and stands at attention]* This doesn't feel right. I am not. I am not … I know that I …

[COLETTE holds out the blindfold by a corner. It hangs down like a signal.]

COLETTE: *Joue!*

[The kerchief is dropped and MARGUERITE falls.]

COLETTE: Captain Bouchardon saw her crumple. He walked over with the others to examine the body. He saw only what seemed like a pile of skirts lying there, a heap of old clothes.

[COLETTE picks up MARGUERITE's violets and exits.]

SCENE TWO

[Sunlight pours in on COLETTE *sleeping at her desk. She is clothed in the kimono-type dressing gown that we saw on the dream* COLETTE *in Scene One.]*

COLETTE: *[Rises, stretches, gets out the kinks, looks out the window, calls the cat.]* Minou. Minou! Come here you little scavenger. You wild little truffle. Ah yes. Ignore me. Twitch your insolent little backside at me. But in your savage little heart you know you want to see me. Ahh! *[Gesture of dismissal]*

*[*HENRI DE JUVENAL *enters the room with a tray of coffee. He is in the uniform of an officer, handsome, poised.]*

COLETTE: Henri! I *thought* I smelled coffee.

HENRI: Annie sent it in. You look as though you've had quite a night of it. Were you up the whole time?

COLETTE: Most of it. I fell asleep at my desk somewhere in the small hours. I had the strangest dreams. You were there.

HENRI: *[Sets down the tray and pours coffee.]* In your dreams?

COLETTE: Yes. But not as yourself. As me.

HENRI: *As you! [Preens a little in the mirror. He is not too pleased.]*

COLETTE: As me, yes. And I was … well, never mind who I was. *[Takes coffee.]* Thank you. *[Sips.]* Oh, it's wonderful. Doesn't Annie know there's a war on? You're not supposed to be able to find coffee like this.

[They sip in silence for a moment or two.]

COLETTE: I suppose you're off for the day.

*[*COLETTE *puts her hands on his lapels and straightens them.* HENRI *shrugs off her touch.]*

COLETTE: It's funny. When you put on that uniform, it's as though you've already left, as though you're already a thousand miles away. Doing battle. Managing the affairs of war and men.

HENRI: I'm only seeing General Gérard. I'll be back by supper.

COLETTE: All the same, you feel so distant.

HENRI: I've merely slipped into my work. You should know about that. When you turn on that little blue lamp I might as well be in China for all the notice you take of me.

COLETTE: You're right, I suppose. *[Pulls his lapel closer to her face.]* Cologne? For Gérard's benefit?

HENRI: For mine. It lifts my spirits.

COLETTE: Makes you feel rakish? Desirable?

HENRI: *[Turns away and spots portrait of Willy.]* Willy. I haven't seen that picture in some time. Going over old times? Wanting them back, perhaps?

COLETTE: Who doesn't want their youth back? But it's not my time with Willy I regret. Nor with anyone else, for that matter. No, I sometimes think the best time of my life was when I lived alone in a single room with no one but my cat to greet me, making do on a crust or two or starving for a few days, with just my pens and paper.

HENRI: And yet, for all your independence, you married again.

COLETTE: It was your body I married you for, Henri, not your wallet.

HENRI: And I thought it was for my cultural status. You've always been a pushover for men with cultural pretensions. Masson, Marcel Schwab. That fellow you pranced about with on the stage, Georges Wague, wasn't it? And Willy, he had it too, that special cultural thing.

COLETTE: *[Sighs.]* Willy. Willy didn't just know culture, he *created* it. He was a pig, a thief, a parasite, an exploiter and yet he was always at the pinnacle. I was afraid to leave him, afraid that if I did I'd fall into some backwater where nothing was happening. It's so ridiculous when you think about it. I was writing the books that made his reputation and yet without him I would have been a nobody. A lot of people would have been nobodies without Willy. Wagner, Debussy, Cesar Frank all owed their success in Paris to Willy.

HENRI: M'sieur Willy, Cultural Impresario.

COLETTE: He was the maestro.

HENRI: A sort of circus barker, I would have said. I think you still are a little mesmerized by Willy, Colette. Your lord and master. Your muse, perhaps.

COLETTE: He was not my lord and master. *[Trying again to touch* HENRI.*]* And he's no longer my muse.

HENRI: *[Turning to the other portrait.]* And this old thing. You weren't bad looking in those days.

COLETTE: And these days?

*[*HENRI *doesn't answer.* COLETTE, *unobserved by him, takes a handkerchief from a drawer, looks at it, and hides it in her hand. She comes back to the portrait.]*

COLETTE: Did I ever tell you about my debut, Henri?

HENRI: At the Theatre des Mathurins?

COLETTE: No, that was my official debut. My real debut took place a year earlier at one of Natalie's Barney's garden parties. Pierre Louys had written a small play and in some misguided moment he asked me to read it. It was a terribly hot day. Thick May sunlight and the air an intoxicating mixture of roses and sweat.

We launched into our little production and suddenly I could see out of the corner of my eye, Pierre raising his eyes to heaven. I knew something was seriously amiss and it didn't take me long to figure out what. It was my accent, of course. My thick Burgundian burl was turning his delicate little rose petals to horse apples.

Of course, once I recognized the problem, the words got thicker and more offensive in my mouth. I just didn't see how I could go on. I prayed to every god in the pantheon: "Get me out of this. Just get me out of this and I'll never say another word in public." Well, the Gods heard me and took pity. In the midst of one of my speeches there was a disturbance at the other end of the garden and suddenly a horse burst out of the shrubbery, a pure white snorting Arabian, bearing a gloriously naked woman.

HENRI: Mata Hari, I take it.

COLETTE: Naturally no one was interested in me anymore. For the rest of the afternoon everyone's attention was pinned on Mata Hari writhing sinuously before an altar in the garden donning and removing drifts of diaphanous veils.

HENRI: Was she good?

COLETTE: She knew how to move. But it was her brass. That was the irresistible thing. The sheer complete brass of her.

HENRI: I've been following her trial in the papers. She's been condemned to death.

COLETTE: One of the scapegoats the military is offering up these days.

HENRI: She's guilty!

COLETTE: It's so difficult for us, Henri! All these readymade roles seem so much more interesting than the ones we can create for ourselves. The unsullied virgin. The ministering wife. The femme fatale. But they must be recognized for what they are. Marguerite was the public's darling once. Now she is their monster. They will hang all their grief on her.

[She turns the picture to the wall and reveals a picture of another COLETTE, *nude under an open kimono.]*

COLETTE: Yes. Our own discoveries, our own images. That's what we must push towards. And if they're ugly, undesirable, they at least will be monsters of our own making.

HENRI: *[Is clearly annoyed with the portrait.]* Is this one of Verté's masterpieces?

COLETTE: You don't like it? I think he's captured me rather well.

HENRI: Rather too well. You're not the spring chicken you once were, Colette.

COLETTE: *[Moves closer and, unseen by* HENRI, *tucks the handkerchief in his pocket.]* Neither are you, my fine scented darling. What's this? *[Indicates the handkerchief which is poking from his pocket.]*

HENRI: What? I've never seen it before. It must be one of yours, or Annie's. *[He gives it to her.]*

COLETTE: Neither Annie nor I have the initials T. G. G ... Not one of General Gérard's, surely.

HENRI: Don't be ridiculous!

COLETTE: Rosewater. Such a delicate scent. Now who do I know ... T ... Her first name wouldn't be Thérèse, by any chance?

*[*HENRI *is jolted, but remains silent.]*

COLETTE: And the G? Could it be ... ? But no. Better to leave it a mystery. Mysteries are so much more delightful.

HENRI: You planted that in my pocket. You had lunch with her yesterday. Don't deny it. I know you did. And who are you to judge me? Fooling with a painter half your age. And don't deny that either. This picture cries out intimate knowledge. Your taste for young men is verging on the scandalous.

COLETTE: Not exactly a taste for young men. More of an interest in a taste for young men. Besides, she's not exactly geriatric, this delicately scented Mlle G. of yours.

HENRI: She is not my ... *[He begins indignantly but, catching* COLETTE's *arched brows, deflates.]* You have it all wrong. There's nothing between us. A little lunch time dalliance. Nothing happened. Come, let's not quarrel over nothing. Annie has breakfast waiting.

COLETTE: No. I feel ready to work. *[Closes the curtains.]*

HENRI: You should have something to eat. Is there anything I can do? Anything you want? *[He moves close to her in an aloof but somewhat appeasing way.]*

COLETTE: Yes. Get Annie to make me one of her chickens. Stuffed with sausage and basted with garlic and thyme. Tell her to make it a fat one, with thighs as wide, as succulent, as Mademoiselle G's. *[Tucks the handkerchief in his pocket.]*

[HENRI pulls away angrily. COLETTE turns to her desk, satisfied that her barb found its mark.]

COLETTE: Something to feed the imagination.

[HENRI exits in anger but COLETTE has already forgotten him.]

COLETTE: And now I must wait. Sit here pondering the pool of light until the thoughts dare to come. They hover at the edge. And, when they see they are welcome, they come sniffing up to be petted. It's a humbling process, Henri. Submitting over and over. Learning the same lessons, the lessons that never seem to stick. Why is it I never learn, Henri? Henri? *[She smiles.]* I see I am alone. Just me and the ghost of Annie's chicken.

I have had more influential muses than a chicken.

[She strokes the picture of Willy and turns it. On the reverse is young man with a kimono draped round his nude body and pearls adorning his throat.]

COLETTE: And muses who were more tender.

[Sits at her desk.]

COLETTE: But few who were as potent.

[COLETTE slips into her working mode, absorbed with her pen and paper, her magic-making in the puddle of light.]

COLETTE: Cheri. Cheri. Cheri. Cheri. Cheri *moves*. He moves like a cat across the window, arched and restless. The sun behind turns him black. Black and thin as a demon in front of a fire. Then, coming away from the light, back to my bed, he turns white again.

[Lights fade.]

Preservation Blues

A jazz piece set in New Orleans

Characters

This play is for five actors:

CASS/NARRATOR, CASS, a photographer
visiting New Orleans

MRS. GAUTIER, proprietor of a bed & breakfast

SHELBY, PIMP, MALE VOICE

STREET MUSICIAN, SHELBY'S NEIGHBOUR

MRS. DEAL, FEMALE VOICE

Setting: An unobtrusive freeform set which enables us to slip in and out of Cass's reminiscences. There is a counter that serves both as a bar and a reception desk to the right, and a settee up stage centre. The musician sits back stage on a high stool. To the front and left is a slide projector, lens facing to the left, which Cass uses to show her slides. The slides, projected on a side wall or curtain, are ephemeral abstractions of colour. The content is in the verbal descriptions, not in the actual slides.

The Male and Female Voices, spoken from off stage, reveal the content of the slides. These may be performed either by the actors who play Shelby and Mrs. Dean as indicated or by separate actors entirely.

Cass slips between her role as narrator and as herself re-enacting the scenes. Her role as narrator is further divided between introspection and actively addressing the audience.

[Saxophone, mournful and lonely, the kind of music that gets under your skin. Lights up on CASS *operating the projector, projecting slides onto some imaginary screen behind the audience. The slides are described by a male or a female voice, sometimes by Cass herself. Spot slowly brightens on the street musician. He is deeply absorbed in his music.]*

FEMALE VOICE: Interior. Night. Street musician in a blue shirt, face and scalp red to the roots with exertion. The spotlight chisels away at him, turning his shirt into slabs of light and dark.

CASS/NARRATOR: *[Pulling her attention from the slide.]* I want to say right up front I haven't taken my best pictures in this town. I don't know why. The material was certainly there but I came away with only a few shots I could sell for a decent buck. And even those … . If it weren't for the edges … .

*[*CASS *advances the slide projector.]*

MALE VOICE: Exterior. Night. An empty street, still shining from the rain, catching the neon bar signs in its puddles.

CASS/NARRATOR: *[Brooding over the picture.]* It's the edge of a picture that interests me most. The part that didn't get drawn into the resolving eye.

You could say New Orleans is like that – the expected front carefully composed for the tourists, but always the sense of something off to the side that's happening in spite of you – something a little chaotic, old secrets, old sorrows, souls breaking into the light, souls slipping back again.

This particular shot, a man was killed here. Right on this spot … . He stepped out of his hotel lobby and was gunned down by a robber.

STREET MUSICIAN: You step into the street ready for everyt'ing the city has to offer and suddenly death takes you. The bright lights fade from your astonished eyes and the music drifts off, sweet, hauntingly familiar … and fading.

CASS/NARRATOR: This shot was taken only an hour after it happened but the street reveals nothing – just that little shadow in the corner where the lamp light doesn't reach.

[CASS *advances the slide projector.*]

CASS/NARRATOR: This is Mrs. Gautier. *[Pause]* Her name was on the Bed and Breakfast list at the Tourist Center.

[MRS. GAUTIER, *a frail woman in her sixties, writes in a ledger at the reception desk.*]

MRS. GAUTIER: I should tell you right now breakfast is *not* included. They never explain that at the Center.

CASS: It's the room I'm interested in, Mrs. Gautier.

MRS. GAUTIER: Well, it's back there across the courtyard, honey. See the stairs to the balcony? That's how you get to it. By the outside stairs.

CASS: It's lovely.

MRS. GAUTIER: We'd given up hope of renting it this evening, Shelby and I.

CASS: Shelby?

MRS. GAUTIER: All that equipment, though. Photographer, are you? I don't know how we'll manage it. Shelby's not himself at the moment.

CASS: Is that Shelby through there? He doesn't look well.

MRS. GAUTIER: He's in the grip of fate, my dear. A contest of major proportions is going on right now in that very room.

[MRS. GAUTIER *readies herself for the camera. Behind her, as* CASS *speaks, we become aware of* SHELBY GAUTIER *stretched out on the settee.*]

CASS/NARRATOR: Mrs. Gautier likes having her picture taken. She takes great care to adjust her hair and the hang of her jacket. But as you can see, her son Shelby, reclining on the settee behind her, is the reason for the picture. Something is going on there. See the pallor of his face, the way his bottom lip is pulled in.

And look – can you see it? That long and bushy shape disappearing round the end of the settee.

[SHELBY *sits up suddenly, looking straight ahead. The spot on him goes out.*]

[*Saxophone music bridge*]

CASS/NARRATOR: Mrs. Gautier is a demon for notes.

MRS. GAUTIER: [*Reading the note as she writes it.*] "The bathroom heater has a one minute delay switch. Turn dial at the bottom of the heater toward the red line and wait one minute."

CASS/NARRATOR: The notes are written in black ink on white card and covered over with see-through tape to preserve them.

MRS. GAUTIER: "When using shower please close the shower door . . .*and* the shower curtain … and please use *both* bath mats."

CASS/NARRATOR: The notes, like Mrs. Gautier, are slender, delicate and a little breathless. It is clear that she regards me as some regrettable force she can never hope to control.

MRS. GAUTIER: "Flashlight, scissors and drinking glasses are in the medium cabinet near the window."

"There are extra towels in the tallboy. Blankets are in wall cabinet nearest the phone."

"Bathroom paper is on top shelf of credenza."

CASS/NARRATOR: The notes are little artifacts of Mrs. Gautier. Signs of her coming and going and perfecting the situation. Training me to the proper use of her room.

MRS. GAUTIER: "*Please* mop up any excess water."

CASS/NARRATOR: The room is dark and cramped but with features that please me – porcelain handles and louvered doors on the cabinets; marble round the sink in the bathroom. There are pictures too, photographs of old New Orleans and a painting of Mrs. Gautier wearing a black gown sprinkled over with white lotuses.

[CASS *advances the slide projector.*]

CASS/NARRATOR: I took this from the balcony. Shelby's wife Unica walking across the courtyard.

It's all there – the swimming, underwater light of the patio, the woman walking through it. Black hair, black shoes, fig black eyes. And that red dress. Every time I see that dress I want to hug myself. She looked up just after I took this … . "I'm meeting a man with badger eyes." Did she really say that? … . I wanted to follow her. I needed … you see she had … . But she hurried down the outside passageway to the iron gate and was gone.

[SHELBY *mixes mint juleps at the bar.* CASS, *camera in hand, is sizing him up as he speaks.*]

SHELBY: I met Unica ten years ago. I was considered a handsome man back then. A bit of a chauvinist with the women. But they didn't seem to mind. You want me here?

[CASS *snaps a shot. There is a touch of the predator in her, an animal stalking its prey.*]

SHELBY: I was living all by myself in typical bachelor chaos. One day I came home to find my house cleaned top to bottom. It was spotless, but there was a lingering odor about the place I couldn't identify. Something like a mixture of straw and fur. This happened several times. It was the damnedest thing. I never saw any person, but one time I saw a long red animal slink out through the back gate. I told my next door neighbour about this and he got very excited.

STREET MUSICIAN: Man, you are the chosen one, eh. My uncle in Biloxi, same t'ing happen to him. It's a fox cleaning up your place, a lady fox, and I'm gon' tell you how to get the lady too.

[SHELBY *hands a drink to* CASS, *and sips a little from his own glass.*]

SHELBY: Now isn't this the best julep you ever tasted? It's all in how you use the mint – bruise slightly and savour. The way women like to be treated.

CASS: Not all women.

SHELBY: *[Intimately]* *She* liked it. She couldn't get enough of it.

CASS: I'm not really buying this about your wife. A *fox*, for chrissake.

SHELBY: My neighbour gave me some powder from a bag in his room.

STREET MUSICIAN: What you do is mix it with some clay and salt and spread it across the doorway.

SHELBY: And it worked. The minute she crossed the threshold she turned into a woman.

CASS: Unica.

SHELBY: Unica. She was passionate about me. *[Rueful smile.]* I know what you're thinking. The ruined looks, the red skin, the puffy eyes. But you know, a few years back the ladies couldn't keep their hands off me.

CASS: *[Moving towards him with her camera.]* And now?

SHELBY: That's very close.

CASS: *[Clicking rapidly.]* These are close-up shots.

SHELBY: But will they turn out from this close?

CASS: Uh huh.

SHELBY: *[Moving even closer.]* How about *this* close?

[STREET MUSICIAN strums a washboard rhythm with steel tipped fingers as the lights dim on SHELBY and CASS. They rise again on CASS at her projector.]

FEMALE VOICE: Exterior. Evening. Three tourists with blond frizzy heads hover over their coffee like cabbages in the dark. Beyond them, where the sky is still bright, it is carefree and frantic but here in the foreground the dark crouches, ready to make ghosts of us all.

[CASS advances the slide projector.]

MALE VOICE: Exterior. Evening. Street shot. The iron embroidery of the balconies above. Below, among the coffee cups and hamburger wrappings, a tramp, a discarded person, wrapped in misery, too defeated to move on.

CASS/NARRATOR: That first night I went crazy with the camera. The neon streets. Jazz joints spilling their music into the crowds. People hurrying about, looking for the most important place to eat, lining up for everything.

[CASS advances the slide projector repeatedly.]

CASS/NARRATOR: This is just to give you an idea. All standard shots, though. Nothing worth focusing on.

[CASS stops the slide projector.]

CASS/NARRATOR: This, now. I like this. Preservation Hall. Look at the sweet texture on that wall – a hundred years of mellowing.

[STREET MUSICIAN plays a haunting tune, lovely and tangled, the intricate, simple, essentially holy music of the Preservation Hall Band.]

CASS/NARRATOR: I couldn't get in. I had to stand with the rest of the crowd outside the window nose pressed to the glass. The faces of the people inside were serene and ecstatic, as though the seraphim had touched down for an hour … . Typical tourists. They expect to be enchanted and they get what they expect.

[STREET MUSICIAN segues into raunchy bar music.]

FEMALE VOICE: Exterior. Night Shot. A sallow-faced man in a black suit and cherry red shoes stands in a doorway.

[A PIMP emerges from shadows in cherry red shoes. His demeanor is casual yet expectant.]

CASS/NARRATOR: Don't you love those shoes? Who but a pimp would be caught dead in them. Shoes of a thousand grimy encounters and yet they just shine on.

CASS/NARRATOR: Here's another one of him standing outside a strip joint. Look behind him, over his shoulder there. The red light catching the upturned breast of the dancer. You can't see her face, just the breast and long torso and flat belly and then the shadows.

STREET MUSICIAN: Death come from the dark in red shoes. The shadows have claimed every damn t'ing but these fleeting, tinsel and paste moments. Soon they too gon' slip away.

[CASS *moves with her camera towards the* PIMP, *snapping rapidly.*]

PIMP: How many pictures you gonna take, lady?

[She continues taking pictures.]

PIMP: You come with me I'll show you pictures. Pictures you ain't never seen.

CASS: Those shoes. Those saxophone-gritty-with-longing shoes.

[Saxophone music rises, wild and sexual, gritty with longing.]

CASS/NARRATOR: I had the devil's own time getting the gate open when I got back that night. That's how I reached my room, not through Mrs. Gautier's but by the iron-gated carriage way at the side of the house.

MRS. GAUTIER: "Keys. Going in or going out, ALWAYS turn key towards the main house to open."

CASS/NARRATOR: I couldn't seem to get the key to turn in any direction. I was too drunk, maybe. The derelict lying in the entranceway didn't help. I mean they lie right on your doorstep. You have to step over them to get in your own door … . Of course I had to have a picture of him. Something about the way he was curled into the gate. The composition. This is him. Well. I thought it would be a good shot. But his reaction. You'd have thought I was trying to murder him. He held up his hands in front of his face as if I was beating him. Curled up tighter and tighter into himself.

[CASS *rapidly advances the projector, then angrily throws down the release cable.*]

CASS/NARRATOR: They're all useless! Useless shots!

[Low insistent rhythm on the washboard. CASS picks up release cable and advances the projector once more. Attracted by something, *she halts and backs up the projector.]*

CASS/NARRATOR: Wait! There! Do you recognize her? There in the crowded intersection. Unica. The dress is different, yellow not red, but she's unmistakable … .

[Washboard rhythm]

CASS/NARRATOR: I followed her for hours that morning. An odyssey of light. See how the sun favours her, blowing up her dress into a bubble of amber, laying lozenges of light along her arms and shoulders?

FEMALE VOICE: The eye freezes the world into confections of dark and light.

CASS/NARRATOR: Everything I took that morning was good. And Unica was at the centre of it. I followed her through the Quarter, street by street. She moved with such energy, catching up everything in her path with a joyous scoop. When she came to rest so did I. When she hurried I rushed along behind her like the tail to her kite. When she dipped I fluttered in her wake.

CASS/NARRATOR: We came to rest at the Café du Monde. She was on the market side of the cafe. I was paying for my coffee and beignet when … .

CASS: Mrs. Gautier!

MRS. GAUTIER: You didn't come home last night.

CASS: I did, but it was very late.

MRS. GAUTIER: I had to find you. I need someone to accompany me on an errand.

CASS: Well. It's awkward at this moment. I'm pursuing a line of study right now that's most … compelling.

MRS. GAUTIER: My errand is also compelling.

CASS: Perhaps later this afternoon.

MRS. GAUTIER: It's compelling and dangerous. That's why I need a companion.

CASS: You're in danger, Mrs. Gautier?

MRS. GAUTIER: I'm going to see a lady of great power, so much so that even the trip there and back is *fraught* with peril. I have need of someone strong and youthful.

CASS/NARRATOR: The sun was not kind to Mrs. Gautier. It cast a green light on her face, adding a bluish touch to the lips. It made a joke of her scrawny legs and arms. For a moment, pitying her, I faltered, about to give in. Then my quarry fluttered up from her table on the other side of the cafe and moved into the market.

In a flash, I was up and moving along with her, pushing my way through the heavy sunlight and the faint odor of corruption, sucking the whole riot of colour and movement into my camera. Then at a vegetable stall among the apples and onions I was arrested by the overpowering and unmistakable fragrance of mint. Bruised mint and Shelby Gautier, his cruel hands and lips, his damaged smile.

The decision seemed almost to be made for me. Unica in her yellow dress moved on and out of my vision. I looked back to Mrs. Gautier. The sun had almost erased her, washed her out to a pale, gravestone white. Even her eyes seemed white.

[Insistent washboard rhythm]

MRS. GAUTIER: Hello! Anyone in?

[MRS. DEAL hurries on stage.]

MRS. DEAL: I'm coming.

MRS. GAUTIER: We're here to see Mrs. Deal.

MRS. DEAL: I've been expecting you.

MRS. GAUTIER: But I didn't make an appointment.

MRS. DEAL: I know all about Shelby and his Unica. Now you all come in to my kitchen and I'll tell you what you have to do.

CASS/NARRATOR: Mrs. Deal brought us into her kitchen. I had been prepared for the apothecary shop of legend. A dimly lit, mysterious cave with potions lining the walls and unlikely things in dusty bottles. But as you can see, Mrs. Deal's kitchen was sunny and cheerful with white cabinets and counters and bright yellow curtains at the windows.

MRS. DEAL: *[Leading* MRS. GAUTIER *to the counter.]* Now you just come over here.

CASS/NARRATOR: That's Mrs. Deal by the counter. She looks more like a boardroom executive than a dealer in spells. That honey-coloured, tailored suit. The little silvery, tightly braided dreadlocks. She looks like an ad for lipstick. Mango peach lipstick. Her voice was smooth as chocolate.

MRS. DEAL: Now before you start asking me for a potion …

MRS. GAUTIER: But that's exactly what I've come for.

MRS. DEAL: Well, I know you been all over town. I know you slipped every concoction known to man or woman into that Unica – love potions, death potions.

MRS. GAUTIER: Never!

MRS. DEAL: Oh, I think so. At least once, maybe twice those potions were intended to … but never mind. What I'm saying is a potion isn't gonna work with Unica. Those potions are for *human* ladies. Now I got something here might work for you.

CASS/NARRATOR: Mrs. Deal opened a cabinet over the counter, revealing an array of white porcelain jars with silver lids and blue labels. Feverfew. Mandrake. Pennyroyal. There were dozens of them. But she wanted something on the bottom shelf. She laid it in front of Mrs. Gautier. It was wrapped in a piece of red silk.

MRS. DEAL: This lady you dealing with is a fox.

MRS. GAUTIER: Oh really! That story Shelby tells. It's a metaphor for his unhappiness.

MRS. DEAL: Unica is no metaphor. What you gotta do is find her skin.

MRS. GAUTIER: I've never seen any skin.

MRS. DEAL: Oh it's there, all right. It's there waiting till she gets the urge to roam. She may already be looking for a new lair.

MRS. GAUTIER: If it's there I'll find it, believe me. It'll go straight on the fire.

MRS. DEAL: No! Don't even consider it. If you let any harm come to that fox skin, misfortune's gonna drop a full load of misery on you. What you need to do is place this little packet inside the skin, right in the belly.

MRS. GAUTIER: What is it?

MRS. DEAL: *[Unwrapping the silk.]* A bone. But not any old bone. It'll do the trick if you do what I tell you. You put this inside and you sew that skin up. How good are you at sewing?

MRS. GAUTIER: I used to be a fine hand with a needle.

MRS. DEAL: Use the smallest stitches you can. Stitch it and double stitch it. Start at the tail end and work up towards the mouth. The last inch or so will be dangerous. You don't want those teeth and claws to get at you.

MRS. GAUTIER: Claws?

MRS. DEAL: Now just two things. You got to open all the windows and doors before you start. You got to leave a place for it to go.

MRS. GAUTIER: For what to go?

MRS. DEAL: Just keep them open. And watch that Unica. She'll try to close them if she knows what you're up to. *[Pause]* The other thing is you don't want this gal here anywhere in the room.

CASS: Me?

MRS. DEAL: You don't want to be anywhere near that skin when it's being sewn up.

CASS: But I don't understand.

MRS. DEAL: You don't understand, then why you doing this?

CASS: I'm not doing this! Mrs. Gautier is. I just came along to give her support.

MRS. DEAL: Uh huh. Well let me tell you, girl, you been making some bad choices lately. You gotta stop getting caught up in those passions.

CASS: What I do is my business.

MRS. DEAL: I'm talking needs not deeds. When was the last time you confessed?

CASS: I don't believe in that nonsense.

MRS. DEAL: If you're smart you'll believe it. If you're smart you'll get yourself to a priest just as soon as you can. And in the mean time, don't go off the beaten track and don't do nothing transformational, you hear?

CASS: Transformational?

MRS. DEAL: You feel any changes coming on, it's too late.

[Washboard]

MALE VOICE: Exterior. Day. Women with painted nails eating po-boys. Dark lashed women with a hint of tinsel in their scarves. Blood red nails picking delicately at the meat of their sandwiches.

FEMALE VOICE: There are two ways to take a picture – with love or with greed. Either way is effective.

[CASS advances the projector.]

MALE VOICE: Exterior. Day. Washboard band. A man with forearms of steel swings his guitar to the sky. A woman strums her washboard with flashy mother of pearl fingers.

FEMALE VOICE: At the edge of the street the bystanders interlock their fingers, blink at the sun, poke through their wallets for dollar bills … And something else Something else at the edge.

CASS/NARRATOR: I wanted a lotus.

[STREET MUSICIAN plays jaunty razzmatazz music.]

[CASS advances the projector.]

FEMALE VOICE: Exterior: Midday. A shack blaring with colour shouts out in ten foot loudspeaker letters "Louis The Duke of Burgundy's Tattoo Parlour!" *[pronounced Burgundy]*

CASS/NARRATOR: Or something like a lotus. A magnolia maybe, something cool and meditative that would rest on my shoulder like a priest's benediction.

[CASS advances the projector.]

CASS/NARRATOR: But Louis the Duke didn't look like a lotus kind of guy. He was skinny and toothless with a devil's goatee and a knitted hat pulled down over his ears. I'll never know why I followed him into that place … But the inside, unlike the Duke, was actually soothing – cool and dim and orderly, with neatly framed tattoo designs hanging on the wall and not the flayed skins of former customers.

[CASS advances the projector.]

CASS/NARRATOR: In the end I settled for a rose. On my left shoulder. This is a shot I took of the design. Very symmetrical. Almost oriental in its peacefulness and symmetry.

STREET MUSICIAN: My uncle in Biloxi, he once did a rose for a sailor, right here on the forearm. The sailor was in love with a girl named Rosalee. The paint's not even dry when the sailor takes up with another girl. Rosalee died soon after that and some say she died of bitterness.

About a month later the sailor comes to my uncle, to see if he can do something 'bout that tattoo. You see it was growing. It had sent t'ree, four shoots winding up his arm and the sailor he swore the t'orns were pricking him. My uncle did his best but for every t'orn he took away two more grew in its place.

A few weeks later word came back to my uncle that the sailor had died in terrible agony. The rose branches had grown around his whole body and the doctor who examined him said he died from loss of blood.

CASS/NARRATOR: I was under the needle for over two hours. And the pain! When he was through, the Duke gave me a glimpse of his work in the mirror, but the mirror was so dirty it distracted me. I suddenly realized how sleazy and how grubby everything was. Who had he used those needles on before? Had he even washed his hands? All I could think of was paying him and getting out of there.

["Long Long Ago" played on a console music box.]

CASS/NARRATOR: *[Dreamily]* They were playing "Long Long Ago" on one of those console music boxes. The music was jangly, far away and sad. The Gautier living room had expanded to a vast size like the ballroom in a gothic novel and it was filled with an eerie blue light. I was wearing an ante-bellum gown – ice blue with scarlet piping. Shelby was standing by the open window with a riding crop in his hand.

Mrs. Gautier was on a gold damask settee. She was dressed in shiny black merino. There was something in her lap, sleek and red with sharp little eyes. I floated over and sat with Mrs. Gautier, steadying the skin as she sewed. Her needle took the tiniest stitches, gathering up the two sides of the belly, sewing them neatly into place. Where she'd already worked the skin was smooth and seamless, so tiny were her stitches.

Just as there was an inch to go, Mrs. Gautier popped the little silk packet into the carcass. Instantly the fox came to life. It writhed and wriggled in my hands and I almost lost it. Mrs. Gautier sewed desperately, trying to avoid those sharp little teeth and claws. Just as she was finishing up, Unica came into the room. She knew right away what was happening. She cried out and headed for the window. But Shelby grabbed her by the shoulders and the fox streaked by them and through the window to the street outside.

[A woman's cry]

CASS/NARRATOR: Unica cried out like a lost soul. She scratched at Shelby with her hands trying to get free. But he overpowered her, pushed her to the floor and lifted his whip. It was then that I saw it wasn't a whip. It was a smoking brand. He brought it down hard on Unica and I felt a searing pain in my shoulder and the smell of scorched flesh.

All this of course was a dream and it was just one of many. Altogether I had a bad night of it, tossing and turning about and getting up for water. My shoulder hurt like the devil and I know I had a fever. Mrs. Gautier came up to my room at seven the next morning. Her hands were heavily bandaged.

CASS: Mrs. Gautier. This is so early. Nothing wrong I hope.

MRS. GAUTIER: Well there is a bit of a problem. Apparently the room is rented out for today. It was booked weeks ago.

CASS: You're kidding.

MRS. GAUTIER: I'm afraid you will have to leave.

CASS: But I've paid for two weeks.

MRS. GAUTIER: There's no record of any payment.

CASS: But I *did*.

MRS. GAUTIER: We're very careful about that sort of thing.

CASS: And I'm not well either. I have a fever and a headache.

MRS. GAUTIER: The Royal is just down the street. You'll get a room there with no trouble. I'll phone them if you like.

CASS/NARRATOR: I checked out of the Gautiers' in a haze of pain and confusion. Apparently I hadn't paid. I thought I had, the very first night, but there was no record and I on my part could find no receipt. Shelby took my money with a slight air of distaste, as though he'd caught me cheating. I had to carry my own bags to the cab.

[CASS advances the projector.]

CASS/NARRATOR: I don't know where this picture came from. I don't remember taking it that morning. And anyway my camera would have been packed. But it must be that morning for you can see the bandages on Mrs. Gautier's hands. And there's Unica. Yes really, that's her on the settee. How defeated she looks. Drained of life. So different to that sun-drenched woman I followed through the market. *[STREET MUSICIAN plays a funeral marching song.]*

CASS/NARRATOR: I decided that the best way to deal with things was to put the Gautiers out of my mind and get back to work.

FEMALE VOICE: Exterior. Midday. A bursting grave. Brick filler pushes through the decaying cement. A corner of the coffin pokes through.

CASS/NARRATOR: You have to do the cemeteries in New Orleans. It's obligatory.

[CASS *advances the projector.*]

MALE VOICE: Exterior. Midday. A blazing white marble tomb contained by an iron railing. A wicker basket full of orange plastic dahlias on the steps.

CASS/NARRATOR: They warn you not to go there alone because of the muggers.

MALE VOICE: The eye separates the quick from the dead.

[CASS *advances the projector.*]

MALE VOICE: Exterior. Midday. Marble tomb with Christ, hands extended in a blessing. He casts no shadow in the noon sun.

CASS/NARRATOR: This was the last picture I took there.

FEMALE VOICE: The eye retrieves things from the edge. Pulls them back into the light.

CASS/NARRATOR: I couldn't go on.

[*Ratcheting sound of washboard.*]

CASS/NARRATOR: All I know is I had to leave.

[*Ratcheting sound of washboard.*]

MALE VOICE: Something off to the side that's happening in spite of you.

CASS/NARRATOR: I had to get away from that … that … .

MALE VOICE: Souls breaking into the light

FEMALE VOICE: Souls slipping back again.

[CASS *advances projector.*]

MALE VOICE: Exterior. Night. An empty street still shining from the rain. Catching the neon bar signs in its puddles.

STREET MUSICIAN: You step into a lamplit street and suddenly death takes you.

[*Ratcheting sound of washboard*]

STREET MUSICIAN: The bright lights fade from your astonished eyes and the music drifts off, sweet, hauntingly familiar . . . and fading.

CASS/NARRATOR: This was shot only an hour after it happened but the street reveals nothing – just that little shadow in the corner ...

FEMALE VOICE: The shadows get under your skin here.

MALE VOICE: There's something off to the side that's going on in spite of you.

FEMALE VOICE: A man with forearms of steel swings his guitar to the sky.

STREET MUSICIAN: Death he come in shiny red shoes ...

FEMALE VOICE: ... skinny and toothless with a devil's goatee.

MALE VOICE: Death in red shoes.

CASS/NARRATOR: I didn't know then that it was too late. I still hoped, I still ran, fleeing anything that was empty, seeking the crowded bars, the jazz joints, the neon warmth and finally that ancient hall where I was swept inside, borne along on the excitement, held up by the crowd as the music began.

Oh that *music*. It flowed and pulsated and filled the hall to the rooftops. Lovely, tangled, intricate, simple, essentially holy, it flowed out and around us, a benison, a salvation, a special prayer. Like sunlight in a rainy street it touched on everyone there ...

... but not on me.

[STREET MUSICIAN *plays a Preservation Hall melody, such as "Good Blues", as the lights fade.*]

NOTES

Production History

Tango Noir was first produced by Maenad Theatre for the 1988 Edmonton Fringe with actors Alexandra Patience and Brian Jensen and directed by Brenda Anderson. In 1991 *Bête Blanche/Tango Noir* was produced at the Pumphouse in Calgary with Alexandria Patience and Don Enright and directed by Gerri Hemphill. Sandi Somers designed the set, and a waltz and a tango were composed by Kevin Labchuk for his soundscape of the play.

Bête Blanche was written specifically as a companion piece for *Tango Noir*. Preceding *Tango Noir* in the performance but taking place later chronologically, *Bête Blanche* depicts a woman, Faye, who is at an earlier stage of self-determination than Colette in *Tango Noir*. The structure in each play is a mirror image of the other, with the whole forming a sort of theatrical diptych on the struggle for spiritual integration.

Preservation Blues was commissioned by the Canadian Broadcasting Corporation as a presentation piece in a radiodrama workshop given at the Banff School of Fine Arts in December of 1995. It was published in *Theatre Alberta,* Winter issue, 1997. In 1998 it was performed as a stage play by the students of Western Canada High as a Drama 30 project, directed by Kari Olson.

Some Thoughts

At the beginning of *Bête Blanche* Faye steals her husband's last dime and his only possession of monetary worth, a silver fitted dressing case. A stolen but beautiful object, it holds forbidden secrets and allurements. Shortly after the theft a sinister ghostlike figure appears who promises to make Faye rich in return for a little attention. Every night the figure brings Faye money and stories of ever-greater corruption. At first it is not entirely clear if this corruption belongs to him or to Faye. But ultimately, of course, it is Faye's.

Faye is that woman we all admired in the old movies – the vamp, the bad girl – because she seemed to be acting by her own lights. But there was always something a bit crummy about those movie vamps. In the end they were not independent agents. They could not make things work for the positive. This was partly determined by the writers who, if they were men, wrote these roles from their particular way of perceiving women, but also because women themselves persisted in accepting the split between "good" and "evil" women.

Bête Blanche is about taking responsibility for one's own fate. The beasts of corruption that women are often hitched to – innocence, frailty, purity – Faye must deal with them if she is to preserve the autonomy of her soul. But by the end of the play Faye is locked in the embrace of Shadow – she has taken on roles and behaviours that have damned her and turned her into a monster.

Tango Noir is a dream encounter between writer Colette and Marguerite Zelle, who was executed for treason October 1917 at the Palais de Vincennes, Paris. Better known as Mata Hari, she had once taken Paris by storm with her exotic dances and more recently had been pursuing a successful, albeit stormy, career as a courtesan. Colette, in whose dream life the play takes place, would have been known to Marguerite as a novelist and actress. Colette too had tried her hand at exotic dancing in a style and costume remarkably similar to Mata Hari's.

As in *Bête Blanche,* the staging of *Tango Noir* is mysterious and elusive, shifting in time and space. The Colette figure, played by a male actor, shifts also though various characters and genders. The action starts with a grappling tango and moves into surrealistic sequences of interrogation, trial and execution.

In *Tango Noir* the responsibility of taking on the shadow is fully grasped. For Marguerite, who never broke free of the entanglements and allurements of the *femme fatale* role, the consequences were fatal. Colette, however, finds a way to cast off the limitations of the vamp persona and appropriate its strengths. She realizes that by doing so she may be perceived as a monster, but she can accept that. "We will be monsters of our own making," she says, suggesting that women must acknowledge the darker side of their natures if they are to have total freedom of action.

In writing these plays I was not suggesting that women should do evil or immoral acts – my thinking was that unless they perceived themselves as capable of the whole spectrum of human behaviors and thoughts they could not make truly moral choices. If you do no evil because you believe that evil is not part of your nature as woman you are prisoner of the persona imposed on you. Only if you resist evil as a choice between behaviors can you be a moral, fully determined human being.

~~~~~~~~~~~~~~~~~~~~~~~~~~~~~~~~~

Preservation Blues is an exploration of some of these same themes of corruption and moral choice. Cass has chosen an exciting, vibrant and creative life but has not come to terms with certain dangers nibbling at the edge of her pictures and her consciousness. She shrugs them off, failing to understand that just because we do not always recognize these choices or are in denial about them does not exempt us from the consequences.

Acknowledgements

My years with the Maenad theatre collective were marked by intensity, high spirits and the serendipitous way that gifted people always seemed to pop up when needed to bring our scripts to life. It is chiefly owing to their generous and inspired contributions to our productions that our plays were able to have a life on the stage. My thanks to all those actors, choreographers, designers, directors, front of house volunteers, musicians, stage managers and crew who worked for virtually nothing to create wonderful stage moments that shimmered for a while but still endure in memory.

I want to thank my colleagues and co-founders of Maenad, Nancy Jo Cullen, Alexandria Patience, Sandra McNeil, Barbara Campbell-Brown and Brenda Anderson, for their inspiration and creativity and for *making it happen*.

And my special thanks to David, who not only supported my theatre ventures in every way possible but made his own creative contribution with brilliant photographs of every production so that those wonderful moments didn't just vanish into the ether but continue to have a glowing afterlife.

ROSE SCOLLARD, a co-founder of Maenad Theatre, Western Canada's first woman-centred theatre, has written over thirty produced stage and radio dramas. In 1996 her play *Shea of the White Hands*, based on the Tristan and Isolde legend, was listed as a finalist for the Susan Smith Blackburn Prize. The following year she was playwright-in-residence at the University of Calgary, under the Markin-Flanagan Distinguished Writers Program, where her play *Caves of Fancy* was workshopped and produced at *Writing Lives*, an international conference on Mary Shelly and Mary Wollstonecraft. In 1998 her children's play *Firebird* was published in TYA 5, a collection of theatre for young audiences; the play was later translated into German by Ute Scharfenberg of Freie Kammerspiele, Magdeburg, Germany, and performed in German as *Feuervogel*. In 2000 she and Caroline Russell King co-authored *Strategies: The Business of Being a Playwright in Canada*.

FRONT COVER: Alexandria Patience as Faye and Don Enright as Shadow in *Bête Blanche*.

BACK COVER: Alexandria Patience as Marguerite and Don Enright as Colette/ Bouchardon in *Tango Noir*.